Assessment and Testing in the Primary School

School Development and the Management of Change Series

Series Editors: Peter Holly and Geoff Southworth
Cambridge Institute of Education
Cambridge, CB2 2BX, UK

School Development and the Management of Change Series: 8

Assessment and Testing in the Primary School

Colin Conner

with contributions from
Doreen Ponting
Margaret Evans
Steve Beynon

The Falmer Press

(A member of the Taylor & Francis Group)
London • New York • Philadelphia

UK	The Falmer Press, Rankine Road, Basingstoke, Hampshire RG24 0PR
USA	The Falmer Press, Taylor & Francis Inc., 1900 Frost Road, Suite 101, Bristol, PA 19007

First published 1991

British Library Cataloguing in Publication Data
Conner, Colin
   Assessment and testing in the primary school. — (School
   development and the management of change)
   1. Primary schools. Students. academic achievement
   Assessment
   I. Title II. Series
   372.1264

   ISBN 1-85000-551-6
   ISBN 1-85000-552-4 pbk

Library of Congress Cataloging-in-Publication Data
are available on request

Typeset in 11/13 Garamond by
Chapterhouse, The Cloisters, Formby L37 3PX

Printed in Great Britain by Burgess Science Press, Basingstoke on paper which has a specified pH value on final paper manufacture of not less than 7.5 and is therefore 'acid free'.

Contents

Dedication

To Sally, James and Charlotte

Acknowledgments

Every acknowledgements section I have ever read always starts with a comment which suggests that the book which follows would never have seen the light of day without the help, advice and guidance of a myriad of other people . . . so it is with this book! My colleagues at the Cambridge Institute have been a formative influence in the thinking embedded within this text, especially Mary Jane Drummond, Marion Dadds, Jennifer Nias and Mel Ainscow. I am also indebted to Geoff Southworth one of the editors of this series who created a conscience to complete the writing, but without making me feel too guilty about not meeting deadlines.

There are many teachers who have worked on courses at the Cambridge Institute whose knowledge and critical comment in inservice sessions has helped formulate my ideas and has given direction to the structure of this publication. I am particularly grateful to Doreen Ponting, Margaret Evans and Stephen Beynon for agreeing to produce the contributions which are included in the text. They illustrate attempts to put some of the ideas discussed into practice. The author would also like to thank the following for permission to reproduce copyright materials:

Sylva, K., Roy, C. and Painter, M. for Appendix A, *Observing Children*. The London Borough of Hillingdon for extracts from their 'Assessment Inset'. Mary Glasgow Publications for permission to reproduce Figure 2.2. Routledge and Kegan Paul for the observation categories of the pupil and teacher records from Galton, M., Simon, B. and Croll, P. (Eds) (1980) *Inside the Primary Classroom*, pp. 12, 13, 17. Deakin University Press for the summary of approaches to studying classrooms from Hook, C. (1981) *Studying Classrooms*. David Hopkins for permission to reproduce Figures 5.2, 5.3 and 5.4 from his book, *A Teacher's Guide to Classroom Research*, (1985). SCDC for Figures 5.6 and 5.7 from Richardson, T., *Approaches to*

Personal Development in the Primary School. Chameleon Books for permission to reproduce pp. 36–8 from Armstrong, M. (1980) *Closely Observed Children*. The Association for Science Education for Figure 6.2 from their (1989) publication, *The National Curriculum — Making it Work for the Primary School*. Oliver and Boyd for permission to reproduce extracts from the checklists for development in Harlen, W., Darwin, A. and Murphy, M. (1977) *Match and Mismatch*. The Isle of Wight Education Authority for Figures 6.5 and 6.7 from their publication (1989) *Topic Work: How and Why*. The Scottish Council for Research in Education for permission to reproduce Figures 6.6 and 7.1 from Black, H., Devine, M. and Turner, E. (1989) *Aspects of Assessment: A Primary Perspective*. Professor Michael Bassey for permission to reproduce the SISTA record sheet for parents in Figure 6.8.

Finally, my grateful thanks to Rita Harvey for coping with continual drafting and redrafting and for being able to interpret my writing.

Colin Conner
Cambridge

List of Figures

Introduction

The terms 'assessment' and 'testing' conjure up all sorts of images in most people's minds. Rows of desks in quiet halls, working to the clock, trying to remember the answers to obscure and sometimes irrelevant questions. Recent invitations to teachers to reflect upon an occasion when they remember being assessed or tested drew up long-forgotten memories of the 11-plus or taking a first driving test. Often these were memories tinged with unhappiness, sadness and a feeling of failure. Assessment for many of us has been an emotional experience and it is not surprising that we should reject facing children with such experiences too early in their lives.

In addition to the emotional nature of assessment, David Satterly, in one of the classic texts on *Assessment in Schools*, suggests that there are two contrasting interpretations of assessment which emerge when many people are invited to explain what they mean by assessment:

> First there is a hard-nosed objectivity, an obsession with the measurement of performances (many of which are assumed to be relatively trivial), and an increasingly technical vocabulary which defies most teachers save the determined few with time on their hands. Secondly, and to many others, assessment presents a very different face as the means by which schools and teachers — sort out children for occupations of different status and remuneration in a hierarchically ordered society. (Satterly, 1989:1)

Each of these views of assessment — as objective measurement, as a means of social classification and as an emotive experience — is suprising when one traces the roots of *assessment*. Satterly traces this to the latin *assidere* — to sit beside. If one combines this with *education*, which can be traced back to the latin *educare* (to bring out), *educational assessment* should be seen as the sitting beside the child and bringing out the potential that exists within them, creating an opportunity for them to demonstrate what they are able to do. Given such a scenario, assessment in education becomes a positive experience, a fundamental feature of teaching and successful learning.

This book is organized around such a view of assessment in education.

The opening chapter is founded upon a basic principle of primary education: that is, to start from where the learner is. This section draws upon views expressed by teachers in recent in-service courses on assessment and indicates some uncertainty about the terminology of assessment. The chapter attempts to suggest that assessment should not be seen as an isolated activity, a knee-jerk response to the requirements of the 1988 Education Reform Act. Instead, Assessment should be seen as an integral part of the means by which a school engages in an evaluation of its role and its success.

The Education Reform Act, especially through the proposals of the Task Group on Assessment and Testing, implies far-reaching changes in the way primary schools, in particular, assess children's progress. The second chapter attempts to explain the proposals and explores the modifications that have emerged since the report was published in 1988. Chapter 3 then offers a critical response to the proposals for national assessment and provides a reflection on the implication for primary schools especially.

Of all the techniques which teachers will need to employ to satisfy assessment of the National Curriculum, observation is the most dominant. It is referred to by the Task Group and included within all the proposals of the consortia working on the development of Standard Assessment Tasks; yet including observation is regarded by most commentators as unproblematic. Chapter 4 explores the skill of observation by teachers and offers strategies to develop observational competence in the classroom.

A central proposal of this book is that, if teachers adopt a research stance in their teaching, it will enable them to collect evidence which will both inform their assessments and support their judgements. Chapter 5 explores additional strategies which can be used as part of the assessment programme to support information gained by observation. In particular, employing the use of anecdotal diaries, audio-recording, video-recording and discussing with children, are explored as ways of gaining access to children's understanding.

Having collected information about children's progress, one of the most pressing concerns of many teachers is how to record it. Chapter 6 suggests that the most effective recording systems are those developed by individual schools that reflect the organization of learning within that school. The section offers examples to illustrate the variations in existence, which others could use to compare and contrast and perhaps modify their own practice.

With the increasing demands of assessment as the National Curriculum becomes established, it becomes even more essential that a whole-school policy for assessment is established. Chapter 7 offers a variety of suggestions to help in the process of developing such a policy. Chapter 8 offers two case studies to illustrate this at the level of the local Authority and the level of the school.

The final chapter attempts to draw the discussion together, emphasizing that assessment should be seen as a positive element of education, a partnership between teacher, learner and the home.

Chapter 1

Exploring Teachers' Views about Assessment

What is assessment?

Why do we do it?

Who is it for?

These three questions have been used as part of a practical activity for groups of teachers in recent in-service courses on assessment. The answers that have been produced are an indication of the age we presently live in. It is an age of accountability, where testing and assessment are central procedures for establishing and monitoring that accountability process. The fact that some educationalists believe that primary schools in the past have not been particularly effective in this area is demonstrated by a recent comment from the Chief HMI Eric Bolton, who suggested:

> In secondary education there is a long history of debate and practice in respect of both the curriculum and examinations. Neither is as true of primary eduction. It is difficult to identify sufficient common ground, or at least common language, to begin to discuss the primary curriculum nationally, let alone carry out the kind of scrutiny and development required to establish a primary curricular framework and agreed objectives. (Bolton, 1985: 36)

Assessment and testing should not be seen as an immediate response to such critical comments, however, but as a central feature of the teaching and learning process. By careful consideration of assessment procedures we can improve children's learning experiences as well as satisfy the demands of accountability. However, more of that later. To return to the three questions posed at the head of this chapter, the responses of teachers to them have been wide-ranging, as can be seen by what follows. As far as the first question is concerned, a variety of responses have emerged.

What Is Assessment?

— 'It's to do with testing'
— 'How good you are at something'
— 'I use it to keep a check on my children, by spelling tests, table tests and things like that'
— 'It's like going back to the 11+ all over again; hoops for the children to jump through'
— 'Assessment is an on-going process which focuses on the whole life of our school. "Are we being effective?" is the central issue and one of increasing national importance'
— 'I feel as though it's a big stick hanging over our heads, teacher appraisal and all that'
— 'Diagnosing strengths and weaknesses'
— 'I use tests in my classroom. I also use quizzes — as a way of keeping a check on the children's learning. I also mark their work, sometimes with a grade but usually a comment'
— 'Our LEA does our main assessment with tests at 7 to check up on children's progress in maths, English and reading to see who needs extra help'
— 'Assessment is to do with record-keeping: information about how well the children are doing'
— 'Isn't it something to do with evaluation?'
— 'The Educational Psychologist does most of our formal assessment. He's very difficult to get hold of though!'

Reflection upon these comments, which are fairly typical, indicates a confusion particularly about terms such as assessment, evaluation, appraisal, testing and accountability, all of which are part of the full assessment picture, as it is hoped later sections of this book will demonstrate.

Many of the interpretations represented in the teachers' comments are included in the definition of assessment offered by the recently established Task Group on Assessment and Testing (affectionately known as TeeGAT), where they described assessment as:

A general term enhancing all methods customarily used to appraise performance of an individual pupil or a group. It may refer to a broad appraisal including many sources of evidence and many aspects of a pupil's knowledge, understanding, skills and attitudes; or to a particular occasion or instrument. An assessment instrument may be any method or procedure, formal or informal, for producing information about pupils: e.g. a written test paper, an interview schedule, a measurement task using equipment, a class quiz. (DES 1988: *Preface and Glossary*)

Ainscow argues that there is considerable confusion amongst many teachers about the nature and purpose of assessment, primarily as a result of the varied intentions associated with any assessment activity. Assessment, he suggests, can be to do with:

> providing information for colleagues
> recording work carried out by pupils
> giving grades or marks
> helping pupils review their learning
> evaluating the effectiveness of teaching
> helping teachers to plan
> the identification of pupils experiencing difficulty
> maintaining standards
> providing information for others outside the school (e.g. parents, LEAs, employers) (Ainscow, 1988)

With such a variety of potential purposes it is inevitable that the appropriateness of an assessment procedure will be influenced by the original purpose of the assessment and the intended audience of the results.

> In other words, when considering what forms of assessment to use in any situation it is necessary first of all to consider two fundamental questions. These are, 'What information is needed? and, 'Who needs to know?' (Ainscow, 1988)

In their discussions in this area, HMI have suggested that assessment of pupils' work has four main purposes:

1. to provide pupils with an indication of their individual achievements and progress;
2. to help the teacher identify areas of strength and weakness in learning and adjust subsequent teaching in the light of this;
3. to enable pupils to evaluate ways in which they can improve;
4. to show others what standards of work have been achieved. (HMSO, 1988)

Norman Thomas, in another book in this series (1990), has suggested that assessment in primary schools in the past has taken three main forms; *informal assessment, formal processes or tests*, and *summary assessment*.

Informal assessment is that which is continually collected in the course of daily teaching. As Bentley and Malvern comment:

> Teachers make assessments all the time. Sometimes they are full and formal, resulting in a mark, a grade, or a certificate. But they are often a matter of the moment, a check as to who is keeping up with the work, and the reward is no more than a smile or a frown, a nod of the head or an encouraging word...In our view, assessment is part and parcel of the teacher's service to pupils, not merely as motivation and reward, but as a direct contribution to the children's growing awareness and appreciation of themselves. (Bentley and Malvern, 1983)

The second kind of assessment identified by Thomas describes *the more formal exercises* undertaken by children, which are devised and set by the teacher, or by people who may never have seen or worked with the children. He suggests that:

> When they are set, the teacher and children know that the occasion is special in that the process of teaching is abandoned for the time being. The children must rely on their own resources and expect no help. (Thomas, 1990)

Some of these procedures are likely to be 'standardized' either by the format being undertaken in a prescribed manner, or the results being compared with a group chosen to be representative of a wider population of children often of a similar age or aptitude.

The final category identified by Thomas describes those attempts to draw together perceptions of children's progress over time — i.e. over a week, a term or a year — and when these are entered into some kind of *permanent record*.

Thomas also offers an additional category, which arises from developments in National Curriculum assessment. The standard assessment of the National Curriculum, he suggests:

> ...ought not to look like tests to the children and should, like teachers' informal assessments, be concerned with identifying what children can do...In some ways they may look like mini-schemes of work. They will be standardized in the sense that they should be presented and marked in prescribed ways. (ibid.)

Further detail as to exactly what is included in assessment comes from Macintosh and Hale (1976), who suggest that teaching and assessment are inseparable and include all or some of the following elements: diagnosis, guidance, grading, selection, prediction, and evaluation.

Each of these characteristics was represented in the teachers' responses to the other two questions raised earlier: *why do we do it?* and *who is it for?*

Why Do We Do It?

It can further improve the effectiveness of the learning situation by presenting positive feedback to pupils and providing information necessary to ensure continuity at all stages. (London Borough of Hillingdon, 1988)

Teacher responses to the question, *why do we do it?* offered the following typical comments. An attempt has been made to classify each of them using the criteria identified by Macintosh and Hale:

'To evaluate our planning and the effectiveness of our teaching.' (evaluation)
'For reinforcement and feedback to the children, so that they know how they're getting on.' (diagnosis and guidance)
'To know where we are going.' (guidance/prediction)
'To find out what and how much children are learning; an indication of their progress, and how they compare with others.' (diagnosis, grading)
'To know what to do next.' (prediction, selection)
'Diagnostic — to highlight strengths and weaknesses.' (diagnosis)
'To aid continuity, provide information for the next teacher and ensure a broad, balanced curriculum.' (guidance, prediction)
'As a form of self-evaluation about one's own teaching.' (evaluation)
'To provide information for the parents about their children's progress.' (evaluation)
'To satisfy legal requirements, in the future especially. It's part of a school's accountability.' (evaluation)
'For some of our children, I have to admit, it is to help them move to independent schools.' (selection)

Thomas endorses many of these suggestions and identifies four main purposes of assessment:

1. to inform the current teacher and to enable him/her to decide what a child should do next;
2. to inform the children about their own progress;
3. to inform others about the progress of individual children (e.g. parents, the next teacher(s), educational psychologists);
4. to provide information for the public. (Thomas, 1990)

As far as the first purpose is concerned, Thomas reminds us that informing the teacher about the next stage in learning is a highly skilled activity and is more complex than we realize. He illustrates this by discussing the implications for the child who has demonstrated that s/he can do what is asked. He suggests that three possible reactions emerge from such a diagnosis. We can offer the child more of the same, a response which has led HMI and others to comment that children are often doing work which is insufficiently demanding. Alternatively, we can provide the child with more difficult work of the same kind, inviting the use of skills and ideas already developed and as a result extending them. Another course of action is to decide that the evidence confirms the child's competence and move him/her on to something quite different. Careful assessment helps us make these decisions more effectively.

The second purpose described by Thomas recognizes the important role of the learner in his/her own assessment. After all, whose learning is it? As Hewett and Bennett comment:

> It is as pupils take responsibility for their own learning, understanding what is required of them, setting their own realistic goals, evaluating their own performance in the light of them, that motivation and that all important ownership is improved. (Hewett and Bennett, 1989)

With regard to informing others, parents in particular, the ILEA report, *Improving Primary Schools* reminds us that parents require assessment information of two main kinds:

> When parents ask teachers how their children are getting on they often have two different questions in mind. They want to know whether the child is working well and making the progress of which he or she seems capable. They also want to know how their child is getting on compared with others of about the same age. Teachers' inclinations are to answer the first question but to be less interested in or even fearful of the consequences of answering the second. They may think that the parents want to push their child on unsuitably, or that they will be wrongly depressed if the child is, in some sense, slower than his or her contemporaries. (ILEA, 1985: par. 2.255)

The report went on to argue that parents have a right to answers to both questions, but that they need to understand the parameters within which the answers are set. Most parents do see their children's work, but there was also a recommendation that parents be able to see how their children stand in relation to others, not necessarily by direct comparison with their peers.

A possible solution would be to have available anonymous examples of work from children of different ages and showing the spread of achievement currently found. There is no reason why such a collection should be limited to written work; it could include mathematics, drawing and painting, models and tape-recordings of children reading. The purpose would be to show the range of achievement that might reasonably be expected from children of different ages not, as is more usual and right for other purposes, to show work of high quality to raise teachers' expectations. (ILEA, 1985: par. 2.257)

With regard to the fourth purpose of assessment identified by Thomas, we move on to the final question asked of the teachers on the in-service course referred to earlier: *Who is the information for?* Thomas suggests that, more recently, information on asessment appears to be to inform the public, but he recognises a variety of other potential audiences. For example, he suggests that assessment information should:

provide elected members and possibly the public with information about the quality of education in the authority's area;
provide information that will help in the transfer of pupils from primary to secondary school;
influence teaching;
identify schools with unsatisfactory achievements;
identify children who are failing and who need extra help.

Some of these were alluded to by teachers.

Who Is It For?

ourselves and other colleagues (evaluation / guidance)
parents (guidance)
the children (diagnosis / prediction)
governors (evaluation)
Local Education Authority (evaluation)
future schools (selection / guidance / prediction)
the Department of Education and Science and the Government with the National Curriculum (guidance (evaluation)

It is also possible to take this set of questions further by relating *why* we assess to *what* and *how* we assess. A study by Black *et al.* of assessment practice in Scotland produced the following example when one school engaged in this activity:

WHY DO WE ASSESS?
1. primarily to aid the child's development
2. to provide information for class teacher
3. to provide information for promoted staff
4. to provide information for other staff — learning support/specialist
5. to provide information for outside agencies — child guidance/other primaries, secondaries etc.
6. to provide information for parents

WHAT DO WE ASSESS?
1. acquisition of knowledge, concepts and skills
2. ability to apply the above to new situations
3. communication skills (with variety of audience and in variety of ways)
4. attitudes

HOW DO WE ASSESS?

1. THROUGH OBSERVATION — formally (as in practical activities and problem solving)
2. THROUGH ORAL WORK — direct questioning interview with child
3. THROUGH WRITTEN WORK — direct questioning
— extended writing
4. THROUGH TESTING — informal (teacher constructed)
— formal (diagnostic/norm referencing) (Black *et al.*, 1989)

Similarly, Duncan and Dunn suggest that assessment in primary schools focuses upon:

the acquisition of knowledge, concepts and principles
the ability to apply concepts and principles to new situations
the ability to communicate
the ability to solve problems
the development of attitudes (Duncan and Dunn, 1985)

They go on to suggest that the usual forms of assessment include some or all of the following:

Children: writing activities (extended, sentence-completion, multiple choice — words and numbers);

drawing activities (pictures, diagrams, maps);

oral and aural activities;

physical/behavioural/performance activities (showing understanding by doing);

self-assessment activities (profiles).

Teacher: informal assessment as a normal part of classroom routine (marking, listening, talking, discussing);

formal assessment via tests, quizzes, structured activities, published tests, inventories, rating scales and checklists;

observation. (ibid.)

If you had asked any of these questions: *What is assessment? Why do we do it? Who is the information for? What and how do we assess?* of primary teachers ten years ago, many of the responses described above would certainly not have been included. There is a clear recognition in the comments cited of the likely involvement nowadays of parents, pupils, governors, LEA and central government in our reflections on assessment, a point succinctly emphasized by Colin Hook:

Teachers today are being held increasingly accountable for their pupils' progress, and classrooms have become more public places and open to examination with the progressive involvement of parents and community bodies in curriculum planning and development. (Hook, 1985: 4)

As was suggested earlier, however, assessment should not be seen as an isolated activity. It is an essential element of teaching and learning, and contributes towards the effectiveness of any school. Assessment is an ongoing process and an integral part of the educational experience of each child. It is through the careful selection of learning experiences and decisions about the most appropriate means of monitoring those experiences that progress is maintained. As Ainscow has suggested:

. . . assessment . . . should be a continuous process of gathering and reviewing information in order to help pupils succeed in the classroom. (Ainscow, 1988)

In establishing a routine for considering how assessment might become a regular feature of our planning, we are likely to contribute significantly to children's progress, but also improve the quality of learning provided by the school as a whole in the process.

This is recognized in comments from the Gulbenkian Report, *The Arts in Schools*, where it is suggested that:

. . . the form and method of assessment should vary with the activity and the type of information sought. Assessments of pupils are not, nor can they be, statements of absolute ability. They are statements about achievements within the framework of educational opportunities that have actually been provided. In some degree every assessment of a pupil is also an assessment of the teachers and of the school. (Calouste Gulbenkian Report, 1982: par. 130)

As a result of this, the report went on to argue that schools need constantly to review the quality of their educational provision and their methods of work; that is, to engage in a process of educational evaluation, which is seen as:

. . . a more general process than assessment in that it looks beyond the pupil to the style, the materials and the circumstances of teaching and learning. If teachers need to assess pupils they also need to evaluate their own practice. Although they have different purposes, assesment and evaluation are obviously linked. Teachers and pupils alike need information on each other's activities and perceptions if their work together is to advance. Assessment and evaluation should provide this as a basis for informed description and intelligent judgement . . . (ibid., par. 131)

The diagram below (Fig. 1.1) demonstrates the inter-relatedness of the ideas raised so far, i.e. that assessment is a central feature of the teaching and learning process; that it is part of our continual evaluation of the effectiveness of our school; and that, in turn, this is part of the accountability process. By implication, it means that planning for

Figure 1.1: The interrelationship of Teaching, Learning, Evaluation and Assessment

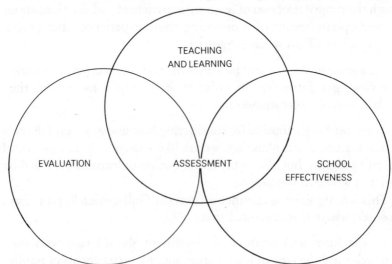

assessment requires consideration of national and local expectations as well as immediate school needs and the concerns of individual pupils, if an appropriate assessment structure is to be established.

The interrelationship of such issues and their role in the developing school have been addressed in the introductory text to the series of which this book is part (Holly and Southworth, 1989).

The importance of serious consideration of these issues has become more prominent with recent developments in the United Kingdom in terms of a National Curriculum and its associated procedures for assessment and testing. The next chapter goes on to describe the basic features of the assessment proposals, and develops further our understanding of the nature of the assessment process. The activities described below may help you in starting to think about assessment. The first two draw upon issues already raised. The matrix offered as activity 3 is a modified form of an idea developed by the London Borough of Hillingdon's assessment team.

Activities

1. How would you or your colleagues react to the questions posed during this chapter:

> What is assessment?
> Why assess?
> Who is it for?
> What do we assess?
> How do we assess it?

2. What goes on in your school at present that can be explained through the categories of assessment defined by Macintosh and Hale; i.e., diagnosis, guidance, grading, selection, prediction and evaluation:

> diagnosis
> guidance
> grading
> selection
> prediction
> evaluation

3. Where are we now?

The following statements reflect differing oppinions about assessment. They might be a useful strating point to explore current practice in your school or classroom.

ITEM	All the Time	Sometimes	Never
I/We use marking to correct children's errors (of content, of presentation)			
Children understand the ways I/we assess them			
Marks or grades are the main way I/we assess children			
I/we use comments as the main way of reporting assessment to children			
Reports are written by teachers for the parents			
Negative comments are included in our reporting to parents			
Negative comments are included in our reporting to children			
Children are encouraged to set their own learning targets			
Children are given opportunities to comment upon their work			
Reporting/recording focuses upon the development of children's skills			
Reporting/recording focuses upon the development of children's knowledge			
Reporting/recording focuses upon the development of children's understanding			
Reporting/recording focuses upon the development of children's attitudes			

ITEM	All the Time	Sometimes	Never
Assessment, recording and reporting include negotiation between children and teachers			
Children are encouraged to attend parent-teacher consultations			
The emphasis in assessment is on success			
Reports/records are written at predetermined times during the year			
The reporting procedure compares each child with others in his or her class/age group			
Marking and assessment are designed to indicate children's strengths			
Marking and assessment are designed to indicate children's weaknesses			
Parent-consultation evenings take place at set times each year			
Marking and assessment procedures are designed to motivate the children			
Children are invited to assess themselves and their progress			
Children are invited to assess each other's work			
There is a common policy for assessment in my school			

Chapter 2

Assessment, Testing and the National Curriculum

Despite the bewildering times for education in which we live, it is probably true that nothing has caused greater consternation amongst the ranks of teachers than the Government's proposals that children should be tested at the ages of 7, 11, 14 and 16. The Task Group Report on assessment and testing for the National Curriculum was published in 1988. Much to the surprise of many, the report was considerably more ambitious and much more forward-looking than was anticipated, and included suggestions with potential for the improvement of children's learning experiences and more successful monitoring of their progress. The report endorsed many of the issues raised in the previous chapter. For example, a central feature of the report is that assessment should be seen as *formative*, which means that it should provide information to the teacher which will influence the organization and structure for future learning both for the individual child and the class as a whole.

Formative assessment contrasts with most of our experience of assessment, which tended to be at the end of a learning experience. We were often given the results of our test or an exam at the end of a course. This is *summative* assessment, and although it is still an element of the assessment proposals it is recognized as being of less importance, since formative assessment is more likely to contribute to extending the learning process. Lincoln and Guba (1981) have suggested that formative assessment is concerned with 'refinement and improvement'. Anne Qualter clarifies this when she defines formative assessment as a procedure that:

> provides information on the achievements of individual pupils
> which will assist in the planning of the pupils' future work. This
> requires the use of as wide a range of assessment modes as possible.
> The basis for the development of such tasks is the description of
> clearly defined attainment targets. (Qualter, 1988)

Formative assessment has a number of typical characteristics. It tends to emphasize the positive, focusing upon what the child is able to do, what he or she knows or understands. It provides the teacher with information that influences future learning and provides real feedback to the pupils. It often involves the pupils in a dialogue about their experience and understanding, and contributes to their taking more responsibility for their own learning and progress. In this context is often identifies areas for improvement on the part of the pupil and at the same time helps in the process of evaluating the curriculum.

The third central feature of the TGAT proposals is that the *diagnostic* purposes of assessment should be recognized, through which learning difficulties might be scrutinized and classified so that appropriate remedial help and guidance can be provided.

TGAT also recognized that a major purpose of assessment was *summative*, recording the overall achievement of pupils in a systematic way. Summative assessment, Guba and Lincoln argue, is concerned to determine the impact of outcomes of learning. As Qualter suggests, it should:

> provide information about achievement of a pupil on some well-defined aspects of the curriculum. (Qualter, 1988)

The discussion of purposes in the report also regards the *evaluative* nature of assessment as being of considerable importance, since it provides a means by which some aspects of a school, an LEA or other discrete parts of the educational service can be assessed and/or reported upon.

The report emphasized the importance of building on existing good practice:

> Promoting children's learning is the principal aim of school. Assessment lies at the heart of this process. It can provide a framework in which educational objectives may be set and pupils' progress charted and expressed. It can yield a basis for planning the next educational steps in response to children's needs. *By facilitating dialogue between teachers, it can enhance professional skills and help the school as a whole to strengthen learning across the curriculum and throughout its age range.* (DES, 1988: par. 3)

A final major element of the proposals is emphasized in the last sentence, and focuses upon moderation and reinforces the potential benefits of participating in such a process. As Joan Dean suggests, one way of improving our understanding of children's learning, and thereby our assessment of that process, is to engage in reflection with other teachers, who:

> ... because they are different people, will see differently from you and may thus enlarge your seeing. (Dean, 1983)

The moderation process has two main functions, according to the report: to communicate general standards and to control deviations from general standards by appropriate adjustments. The procedure advocated by the Task Group is that of *group moderation* where the emphasis is on . . . 'communication through discussion and exchange of samples at a meeting'. (DES, 1988: par. 72)

This process will allow teachers to clarify their judgments by having to explain them to others and in doing so reveal the basis of their assessments. This, it is argued:

> . . . would enable the professional judgements of teachers to inform the development of the national curriculum. (ibid.: par. 75)

The value of group moderation lies in the emphasis on communication and the need to make the basis of our judgement more explicit. It provides teachers with the opportunity to discuss possible interpretations of pupils' learning experiences.

> Mismatches between internal and external assessments can be discussed in terms of the interpretation of the National Curriculum and the effectiveness or otherwise of national assessment instruments. These professional deliberations have a valuable staff development function while at the same time, with appropriate documentation of decisions, providing formative feedback to the relevant subject groups concerned with the development of the National Curriculum. (ibid.: par. 76)

A further feature of the report is the emphasis on 'criterion-referenced' rather than 'norm-referenced' assessment:

> The assessment system being proposed differs from most of the standardized testing that is now used in many primary schools and some secondary schools. Those tests are not related closely to what the children are being taught, and when they identify children likely to have difficulties they give little indication of the nature of their problems. Their purpose is to compare children with each other and with samples of children with whom the tests were originally developed, often many years ago. (ibid.)

Such traditional tests are described as 'norm-referenced'.

What the Task Group recommend, however, are assessments which are 'criterion-referenced' — much more like the assessments teachers make about children every day. The definition of criterion-referenced assessment offered in the report is:

> an assessment system in which an award or grade is made on the basis of the quality of the performance of the pupil, irrespective of the performance of other pupils; this implies that teachers and pupils

be given clear descriptions of the performances being sought. (ibid.)

So it is intended that each child's progress should be viewed primarily in relation to him or herself, and that s/he be provided with information on what the assessment is about.

The differences between norm- and criterion-referenced assessment are usefully summarized by Croll when he suggests that:

Many discussions of assessment tend to emphasize the greater educational value of criterion-referenced assessment compared with norm-referenced methods. Norm-referenced testing has been criticized for imposing a purely statistical model of academic achievement. Using norm-referenced methods, whatever the overall level of achievement, some children must always be top and some bottom. Standardization against population norms means that approximately half of a population must always be below average, however well they perform. Such methods are also criticized as being of little educational value; to know that a child is 18th in the class or in the top quarter of the population has no obvious implications for teaching, and test items may be selected on the grounds that they spread out performance rather than for their educational interest. Norm-referencing has also been criticized for being elitist and obsessed with differentiating children and sorting them into a hierarchical ranking.

In contrast, criterion-referenced testing can be seen as being concerned to tell teachers what they need to know through concentrating on whether particular curriculum objectives have been met. And the content of criterion-referenced items are more likely to relate to the actual content of what teachers are trying to assess. (Croll, 1990: 9)

Figure 2.1 describes some of the major differences between norm- and criterion-referenced testing.

The National Curriculum as proposed now includes eleven foundation subjects of which the first three are to be core subjects (i.e. English, mathematics, technology, history, geography, art, music, PE, a foreign language and, more recently, RE).

Working groups have been established for the first six areas and have proposed or will be proposing attainment targets for the 5–16 age-range. Notes of guidance are to be issued for the remaining areas, and RE is to be based upon the existing agreed syllabi.

If detailed assessment were undertaken from the above list of subject areas, teachers would be spending all of their time in assessment. To overcome this the Task Group recommended:

Figure 2.1: Criterion-referenced and Norm-referenced Assessment

Criterion-referenced Assessment	Norm-referenced Assessment
— concerned solely with an individual child's performance on a specific task	— concerned with comparing performance of a child in some 'ability' area with that of a peer group
— directly related to teaching objective set by the teachers — related to the curriculum	— related to a hypothetical notion of ability determined by the test constructor — unrelated to the curriculum
— provides explicit information on what the child can and cannot do; what he or she needs to be taught	— results often have few teaching implications
— can be undertaken in normal teaching situation	— requires formal standard test conditions, often removed from the classroom
— can be repeated (e.g. daily)	— usually a one-off activity
— provides a basis for continuous monitoring of a child's performance in school; can be a natural part of a child's record	— used in making placement decisions (e.g. Special School) — used in large-scale surveys of educational achievement
— does not involve labelling the child's *performance* is described, not the child	— risks child being labelled as 'of low IQ', 'poor reader', etc
— tests can be brief	— usually time-consuming
— tests can be teacher-constructed	— requires published materials, some of which are unavailable to teachers
— sometimes teacher bias can be present	— often regarded as more reliable and valid

(adapted from London Borough of Hillingdon's Assessment INSET 1989)

> ... the best balance between precision in detail and overall comprehensibility will be found if attainment targets are clustered by subject working groups so that each group identifies about four subdivisions of the subject (never more than six) for reporting ...
> (DES, 1988: *TGAT: A Digest*)

The Task Group described these subdivisions as 'profile components'. For example, in the assessment of science, attention might be given to children's competence in 'observation', 'the identification of hypotheses' and 'the setting up of an experiment to investigate a hypothesis' as examples of three profile components.

Initially, at age 7, each of these would be extremely general, and not necessarily science-specific. They would become increasingly 'science-orientated' when investigated at ages 11, 14 and 16. As a result, some of these components would be appropriate to a number of the subjects in the National Curriculum, others would be much more specific. So in geography, for example, one of the profiles might be concerned with *graphicacy* — the development of children's competence in dealing with information presented in diagrammatic form, as in mapwork.

The Task Group envisage that initially there will be a limited number of profile components at age 7, but anticipate the need to introduce new profile components as the children progress. At the first reporting age of 7 components would tend to be more general than subject-specific, but would be the basis from which later subject components might emerge.

Figure 2.2 helps us to understand the elaboration and extension of profile components as they become appropriate and when introduced as new subject areas.

If we take 'observation' as an example of a profile component and follow the thicker black line in the previous diagram, we see it becoming an element of an increasing number of profiles as we move to testing at 11, 14 and 16.

To investigate competence in each of these profile components the Task Group recommended the use of 'standardized assessment tasks' (SATs). For 7-year-olds, and largely also for 11-year-olds, it was suggested that these should be related as far as possible to the work that is already going on in the classroom. They will be designed so that they look like pieces of work that the children normally undertake, and can be embedded in on-going learning activities.

In the process of doing them, children will be able to demonstrate a range of competence which teachers can monitor by observing the children's activity, the processes they engage in as well as what they produce, whether they be artistic, written or oral. It is anticipated that these teacher-assessments will employ standardized procedures and their results will be moderated by teachers from a group of schools. They will compare and contrast their analyses of their children's responses to the set tasks as well as their own general assessments of children's attainments.

The tasks will be designed and tested in trials to be sure that they can be attempted by the whole age group. Teachers will then be able to select from a 'bank' of tasks those that are suitable for the background and interests of their children, as well as consider the extent to which they relate to the current learning activities of the children.

The suggested advantage of the approach is:

> ...children are much more likely to show what they can really do
> when involved in activities which for them are normal and have a

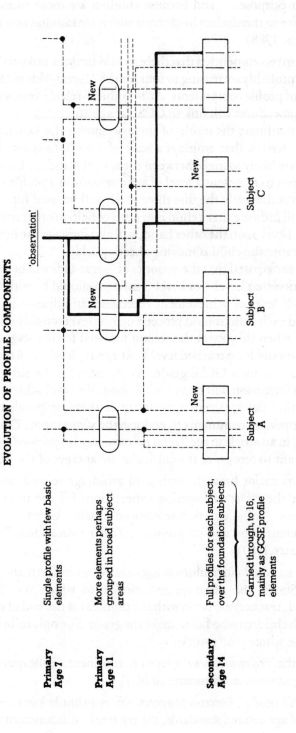

Figure 2.2: Evolution of Profile Components

EVOLUTION OF PROFILE COMPONENTS

'observation'

Subject A

Subject B

Subject C

New

New

New

New

Primary Age 7 — Single profile with few basic elements

Primary Age 11 — More elements perhaps grouped in broad subject areas

Secondary Age 14 — Full profiles for each subject, over the foundation subjects

Carried through, to 16, mainly as GCSE profile elements

clear purpose ... and because children are more likely to do full justice to themselves in contexts which are familiar and interesting. (DES, 1988)

The Group recommended that there should be three tasks at the first reporting age of 7, probably increasing to four for the 11-year-olds to allow for a greater number of profile components. At 14, subject-related tests will predominate, and the procedures will link to GCSE at age 16.

To coordinate the results of this assessment, the Task Group proposed a reporting system that employs a scale of 1 to 10 to cover the progress that children are likely to make between the ages of 5 and 16. Each number from 1 to 10 is seen to represent a level of achievement in a profile component. The intention is that only the first three levels will be used for most 7-year-olds. Level 1 will indicate that a child is in need of help in order to make satisfactory progress. Level 3, on the other hand, will also indicate the need for additional help, because the child is moving ahead quickly.

It is anticipated that the majority of 7-year-olds will be at level 2. There is no intention that Level-1 or Level-3 children should be withdrawn from their class. Each level of achievement represents an advance in knowledge and skills, and each child should proceed up one level roughly every two years. So at age 11 when they meet the second national testing stage, the majority of children should have reached level 4. At age 14, level 5 or 6 means they should well on course for a GCSE grade. At 16, even for the subjects not taken at GCSE, information will be available about the level achieved.

Despite the apparent complexity of these proposals there have been many supportive comments to endorse the suggestions. Dennis Lawton, for example, in an article in the *Times Educational Supplement* has argued that it is important to recognize the curricular advantages of the TGAT model:

> ... its major breakthrough is to avoid age-related norms (which have the effect of lowering expectations for the most able) by a system of criterion-referenced achievement based on differentiation and progression. (*Times Educational Supplement*, January 1989)

Where a national curriculum is age-related, as in Germany, France and the United States, the often-quoted models to which the British system is compared, teachers are faced with the problem at the end of each year of what to do with children who fail to make the grade. The only solution for some is to repeat the whole year's work:

> ... the '*redoublement*' which our continental colleagues have been very anxious to eliminate. (ibid.)

The TGAT model, Lawton suggests, offers a simple but effective alternative instead of age-related standards, the ten levels of attainment described earlier through which *all* pupils will progress, but some much faster than others. This means that a primary teacher working with a class of 7-year-olds will need to be thinking about the curriculum and associated attainment targets across a six-year range. As Lawton comments:

> A major reorientation required of primary-school teachers will be to carry in their minds this stretched (and stretching) curriculum: about six attainment targets in English, 13 in Mathematics and 14 in Science for each of the three levels, i.e. a total of 99 objectives, potentially available for each pupil. (Lawton, 1988)

A major difficulty with this proposal is that it seems to assume that the curriculum is only to focus upon the core and ignores the attainment targets to be generated by the remaining foundation subjects. However, Lawton concludes by suggesting that one of the functions of the standardized assessment tasks will be to help teachers in the process of assessment and differentiation.

A further concern about the proposals has been reporting procedures to be adopted and the extent to which they will lead to divisive comparison between schools. It has been strongly emphasized that information about an individual child should be treated as confidential and available only to the parents. However, it is expected that schools will need to examine the range of levels achieved in each of the profile components and consider whether there are any implications for their programmes of work. Similarly, it is argued that the LEA will need to collect and consider information about the range of results for the schools for which they have responsibility.

Tim Brighouse, former CEO for Oxfordshire, is among many who have criticized these suggestions. He has argued that:

> ... the unremitting and vicarious competition enjoyed by some adults now underpinned the Education Reform Act. The Act gave a higher profile to the 'worst excesses' of competition among children and among schools. (*Times Educational Supplement*, 30 September 1988)

Brighouse instead advocates the use of *ipsative* assessment, by which pupils and schools seek to progress and improve on their own performance. It is of no interest to him that a school in Oxford got better results than a school in South London.

> What matters is that each and every school improves its performance against certain indicators measured against its own previous performance. (ibid.)

The Task Group recommended, however, that there should be no requirement placed upon a school or LEA to publish information about the spread of results of the assessments conducted at the 7-year-olds' reporting stage. At other stages, where they are expected to publish information, the group believes that the results need to be carefully interpreted. They proposed that such information should be made available to enquirers, but:

> ...only as part of a more general statement about the school, produced by the school and authenticated by the LEA. The LEA should also provide material for inclusion in the statement describing the influence of factors, such as the socio-economic nature of the catchment area, on a school's results. (DES, 1988)

A digest of the report concludes:

> The Task Group knows that many teachers are apprehensive about some possible outcomes of a national system of assessment. In brief, there are worries that some pupils may be disadvantaged; that relations between teachers, pupils and parents may be soured; that schools or teachers may be singled out unfairly; and that the process may unduly constrain the work of a school. In arriving at its recommendations, the Group has aimed to prevent or minimize those possible consequences. It has been in no doubt that a successful system of assessment depends upon teachers' confidence in it and their willingness to take responsibility for it. These requirements make it necessary that the system should support teachers' professional concern for the effectiveness of their teaching. The Group is also in no doubt that the system proposed is practicable and that it should contribute to the raising of educational standards by complementing and supporting the work that teachers already carry out. (DES, 1988)

Reactions from Primary teachers to the proposals were initially quite supportive. David Whalley, a member of Cornwall's primary assessment advisory group, commented (1989) that the report encouraged primary teachers to believe that teachers were to play a major role in the assessment process with an opportunity for professional development through the moderation of their assessments via other teachers and a series of pertinent standardized assessment tasks.

Recently, however, the potential merit of these proposals has been brought into question by the recommendations of the School Examinations and Assessment Council (SEAC). Writing to the then Secretary of State, Kenneth Baker, in July 1989, Phillip Halsey, the Secretary of SEAC, proposed a simpler system of assessment and moderation than had been advocated by TGAT. His plans were accepted by the Secretary of State as having, '... the considerable merit of simplicity and comprehensibility.' Instead, SEAC called for a two-tier model.

First, teachers would assess pupils on every attainment target (which means 33 tests for all 7-year-olds in just English, Maths and Science). Subject scores would be aggregated and passed on to local moderators in the Spring.

Second, teachers would administer SATs in the summer to all pupils 'but possibly only for some attainment targets'. Where available, the SAT result would displace the teacher assessment.

Reactions to this proposal were quite vehement, David Whalley, for example, commenting:

> If assessment lies at the heart of the learning process, then teacher assessment lies at the centre of any system. The assessments made by teachers are based upon numerous different samplings over a long period. The assessment is made in the knowledge of the context in which learning takes place.
>
> So long as SATs were to be used in conjunction with teacher assessment, then the system has merit. (*TES*, 25 August 1989)

SEAC's reaction to comments of this kind argued that it was a misunderstanding to suggest that the procedure they advocated undervalued teachers' judgements. In their advice to the Secretary of State dated 12 December 1989, the recommendation for combining teacher-assessment and standard-assessment was as follows:

1. By the end of the spring term preceding the end of the key stage there should be a recorded teacher-assessment giving the level each pupil has reached in each attainment target (a daunting prospect itself).
2. When the SATs have been used in the summer term there will also be a recorded SAT outcome for some attainment targets — probably not all.
3. Where (1) and (2) yield the same outcome for each profile component, that is the end of the matter. The SAT outcome for the attainment target, where there is one, should stand.
4. Where (1) and (2) yield a different outcome for any profile component, the SAT outcome may be used for the pupil record if the teacher is content. If the teacher believes (1) should be used, the teacher will be required to make the case for this choice through local moderating arrangements, details of which still await clarification.

These proposals have been adopted by the Secretary of State and now form part of the final orders for assessment published in July 1990. In addition to prescribing the relationship between Teacher Assessment and Standard Assessment, the orders also contain directions for combining or 'aggregating' the assessment of statements of attainment to produce levels of attainment in the profile components for each of the core subjects and for combining these to produce levels of attainment in each of the subjects themselves. Where a profile component is made up of only one attainment target, as for example in the 'Speaking and Listening' component of English, or the 'Exploration' component for Science, the level for each of these profile components will be the same as the attainment target. Where a profile component consists of four or more attainment targets the level will be the highest level achieved by a child in at least half of the attainment targets involved. For the Writing profile component of English the attainment targets are to be weighted 7:10 for writing 2:10 for spelling 1:10 for handwriting, with fractional scores of half and above being rounded up to the next whole number. (It looks as though we may need a qualification in statistics for this!) A child's level of attainment for each subject is to be based upon an averaging of the results for each profile component, with fractions of one half again being rounded up. In English and Science each profile component is to be weighted equally, whereas in Mathematics, the Number, Algebra and Measures component is to be weighted 3:2 against that for Shape, Space and Handling data.

Initial reactions to these proposals when they appeared in draft form have been one of amazement. Michael Bassey for example, commented,

> The extraordinary feature of this draft order is that it tells how to aggregate profile components into subject scores, and how to aggregate attainment targets into profile components, but does not tell teachers how to aggregate statements of attainment into attainment targets.
>
> It seems that the DES has not recognised that as far as teachers are concerned the national curriculum is essentially about statements of attainment. These are the basic units, not attainment targets nor profile components. It is the statements of attainment which enable teachers to use the national curriculum for *formative assessment* and it is this day-by-day classroom process which can lead to improvements in teaching and thus in learning. (Bassey: Education 6th July 1990, 11)

The next chapter goes on to consider *further* the implications of issues discussed in this chapter for those of us working in the primary school.

Chapter 3

Two Steps Backwards, One Step Forwards? The Implications of Testing and Assessment for the Primary School

Introduction

This school is smart and effective. It doesn't push you too much. You go at your own pace . . . if you stumble . . . well, you get up somehow. You learn a lot because it's so relaxed. I was at a Prep School before. You had tests and exams all the time. All it proved was that you were either good or bad at tests. They never tested what you had learned. I couldn't stand the pressure. I was made to feel a failure every time I asked a question . . . here we talk all the time . . . too much sometimes. (Crowley, 1988)

In the above comment you see a 10-year-old who has already experienced what failure can be like. All that tests had proved to him was that you were either good or bad at them. Fortunately, he is now in a supportive environment where his talents are being developed more fully. But does all testing need to be so negative? By the introduction of national testing with the current legislation (Education Act 1988), are we in danger of developing disenchanted and alienated individuals at progressively earlier ages? Desmond Nuttall has commented, for example that:

The dangers of reinforcing failure from an early age are particularly acute for the disadvantaged, those with special educational needs and generally for those aged 7 (or thereabouts) . . . the experience of testing such young children with national tests is negligible. (Nuttall, 1987)

This is an amended version of an article which appears in Docking, J. (1990) *Alienation in the Primary School*, Falmer Press.

Testing young children often fails to capture their reasoning abilities as the following example by Mehan nicely illustrates:

> Another question instructs the child to choose the animal that can fly from among a bird, an elephant and a dog. The correct answer (obviously) is the bird. Many first-grade children though, chose the elephant along with the bird as a response to that question. When I later asked them why they chose that answer they replied 'That's Dumbo'. Dumbo (of course) is Walt Disney's flying elephant, well known to children who watch television and read children's books as an animal that flies. (Mehan 1973: 315)

Children's answers to questions of this kind can lead to a misrepresentation of their competence.

This has significant implications for primary teachers. In 1967 the Plowden report arued that 'at the heart of the educational process lies the *child*'. In 1984, Richards suggested that the *school curriculum* is at the heart of education, and now we are being told that 'promoting children's learning is the principal aim of schools. *Assessment* lies at the heart of this process' (TGAT, 1987: para 3). Since the demise of the 11 + in most authorities, many primary teachers assume that there is relatively little formal testing going on in their schools and LEAs (a point questioned by Gipps, as we shall see), and that rather than create an atmosphere of competition by excessive testing, their concern should be to create an environment where children enjoy learning without fear of failure. In an article which employed the analogy of creating monsters, Hartnett and Naish commented that TGAT had attempted to take seriously concerns about reinforcing failure:

> TGAT's job seemed not merely to produce general principles governing test construction but to allay fears of well-informed professionals and public opinion about testing. TGAT had to try to show how testing could be both diagnostic and formative (the sorts approved by professionals) and at the same time make possible the benchmark assessment favoured by the New Right (politically), to be used to compare schools and to decide funding. (Hartnett and Naish, 1990:5)

Given such comments, the fear for many primary teachers is that the requirements of National Curriculum assessment means a return to the inequities of 11 + assessment. The Oracle Report reminds us that it is difficult to remember the intense pressure on schools and teachers experienced in the late 1940s and early 1950s related to 11 + selection:

> . . . the league tables that parents drew up for local schools, the

telephoning around to find out who had done well and the sense of failure that some teachers experienced when their pupils won fewer places than others, or than expected; not to mention the effects on the children. (Galton *et al*, 1980: 37)

Primary education within a selective examination-oriented curriculum was influenced to the extent that teachers' intentions, teaching styles and forms of classroom organization were dictated by the need to get results. The present proposals appear to suggest that such conditions might apply from the age of 7. Hartnett and Naish suggest that there are serious doubts as to how testing will bring about the government's anticipated improvements in the education system:

> For a start, the learning patterns of individual children may well not follow patterns susceptible to bureaucratic modes of evaluation. Further, in a culture like that of England and Wales, which is highly differentiated in terms of class, ethnic groups and gender, bureaucratic testing is likely to do particular harm to children from the least privileged backgrounds. The early test-derived labels will stick, and a system of streaming will follow from them. The proposition that testing raises standards is, at best, one hypothesis amongst others, and there are, in any case, great difficulties in measuring standards and changes in them. (Hartnett and Naish, 1990: 5)

This chapter proposes to consider the implications of testing and assessment in the primary school. It opens with a discussion of the increasing trend toward bureaucratization in education, of which assessment is a central feature. This is followed by some reactions to testing generally as a preliminary to a consideration of the implications for primary education. The discussion concludes with a review of some of the more positive features that might arise which have particular relevance for teaching and learning, for, as was stressed in Chapter 1, it is important to recognize that assessment, learning and teaching are inextricably linked. This point is reinforced by Murphy and Torrance, who suggest that

> Wherever learning takes place, or it is intended that it should take place, then it is reasonable for the learner, the teacher and other interested parties to be curious about what has happened both in terms of the learning process and in terms of any anticipated or unanticipated outcomes... good education, by definition, encompasses good assessment. (Murphy and Torrance, 1988)

Education, Accountability and Bureaucracy

Without doubt, we live in an age of increasing accountability. More than ever before, education is likely to be evaluated in terms of its cost-effectiveness and the extent to which pre-specified objectives are achieved. The consultation document, *The National Curriculum 5–16* (1987, DES) was a culmination of this movement and has laid the basis for the 1988 Education Act. Maurice Holt commented that the entire consultation document was:

> ... steeped in the mechanistic assumption that schools can be run like biscuit factories; providing the skills and technology are there, backed by clear objectives and precise assessment, the right product will roll off the assembly line. (*Times Educational Supplement*, September 1987)

But we all know that schools are not like that and that the purpose of education is not merely to prepare children for the work force, especially in primary schools.

Peggy Marshall, a former Chief HMI, at a 1986 Department of Education and Science conference on Evaluation and Appraisal questioned the 'production line', mentality current in the thinking of many politicians. She suggested that, as national economies have weakened and money has become tighter, there has been an increased demand internationally for greater accountability in education, and, given the size of the bill, she believes this is reasonable:

> Often, though, it has been argued in the cost-effective terms of manufacturing industry, with pupils regarded as products off the school assembly line, and their assessed achievement as indices of how far public money has been properly spent.

But such a model, she argues, is inappropriate because, unlike manufacturing industry, which seeks to provide, at minimum cost, a standard product conforming to exact specification with as little variation as possible, schools are trying, within the time and resources available, to develop each individual as fully as possible.

> The more successfully it does so, the more divergent, beyond certain basic competencies, the pupils are likely to become.

The Government have argued, however, that a major problem to be faced is whether

> ... we are giving so much freedom to each individual school that

continuity for our pupils in a mobile society is ignored...
(*Schools Council Working Paper No. 33*, 1971)

and that

there is a need to improve relations between industry and
education. (*Education*, 22 October 1976)

Tremendous changes have taken place in the world of work since the
mid 1970s, and this has had a profound effect on education, especially in the
secondary sector. We cannot be sure, however, exactly what kinds of
employment children currently in primary schools will undertake, or even if
they will have full-time employment at all. Issues of this kind strike at the
very purpose of education: should it give children a good general
foundation, or should it prepare them for specific careers?

The Secretary of State for Education, at the North of England
Conference in January 1987, described the English education system as one
of those institutionalized muddles that the English have made peculiarly
their own! He went on to introduce the well-worn comparison with our
European competitors:

In England we are eccentric in education as in many other things.
For at least a century our education system has been quite different
from that adopted by most of our European neighbours. They
have tended to centralize and standardize. We have gone for
diffusion and variety. (Baker, 1987)

In a second speech in January 1987, to the Society of Education Officers,
Kenneth Baker introduced a criticism of those professionally involved in
education:

I realize that the changes I envisage are radical and far-reaching
and may, therefore, be unwelcome to those who value what is
traditional and familiar and has often served well in the past. But I
believe profoundly that professional educators will do a disservice
to the cause of education, and to the nation, if they entrench
themselves in defence of the *status quo*. More and more people are
coming to feel that our school curriculum is not as good as it could
be and needs to be, and that we need to move nearer to the kind of
arrangements which other European countries operate with
success, but without sacrificing those features of our own
traditional approach which continue to provide their worth. (ibid)

Yet not everyone agrees with the suggested advantages of the education
systems of our European competitors. Broadfoot and Osborn, in their

comparative study of French and English School systems, found French primary schools were typified by '. . . a dull, repetitive and harsh pedagogy', and they suggest that teaching to a prescribed curriculum and national tests would lead to the loss of

> . . . that warm and creative learning environment that has made English primary schooling the envy of many parts of the world. (Broadfoot and Osborn, 1987)

On entering secondary school, one in three French children is older than his or her classmates as a result of having had to repeat some of their primary schooling. In fact the number of *redoublements*, children having had to repeat a year of their schooling, has more than doubled during the past decade. In 1975 the fifth grade (aged 12) had to be repeated by 6.5 per cent of pupils; by 1985 this had increased to 16.5 per cent.

Michelle Rey, a French student at the Sorbonne who spent some time visiting English comprehensive schools, wrote in an article comparing French and English schooling:

> In both schools, different as they were from each other, the atmosphere is much warmer and more cordial than in our continental schools. British pupils seem to get much more satisfaction from their school days than do their French fellows. For instance, children's paintings are rarely displayed at our secondary schools, where punishment occurs more often than encouragement or praise. Indeed, it is generally believed by French educationists that pupils must understand that study is for their own good and no reward for their efforts should be expected. (*Times Educational Supplement*, October 1988)

It is also the case that, in France, attempts have been made to introduce devolution in the government of education, motivated by the need for 'more flexible, locally relevant, educational provision at a time of significant social and economic change (Broadfoot, 1988). Broadfoot also suggests that a history of centralization in France has created teachers who are conservative with no enthusiasm for, or experience of, teacher-led development at a time when this is felt to be urgently needed.

Similarly, in the West German system, so much admired by our DES, Chisholm reminds us that

> . . . pupils are under great pressure to achieve demonstrably and continuously . . . children gradually learn to see grading as a process of personal affirmation. (Chisholm, 1987)

In such a situation, the able survive, but there are significant numbers who do not. Even the United States, where testing is used extensively,

> ... appears to be moving away from such reductionism towards promoting the culture of the individual school, a more liberal approach to curriculum experience and a more professional, highly paid and liberally-educated teaching force. (Holt, 1987)

There clearly seems to be a difference of opinion between those who are professionally involved *in* the system at present and those who have a bureaucratic responsibility *for* the system.

Clyde Chitty describes the differences between these two groups as follows: the professional approach, he suggests,

> ... reflects a genuine concern with the quality of the teaching process and with the needs of individual children ... It requires teachers who are well-motivated, well-trained and skilled in identifying any specific learning problems for individual pupils. It is wary of any system geared to writing off large sections of the school population as failures. (Chitty, 1988)

The bureaucratic approach, on the other hand,

> ... is concerned with the efficiency of the whole system and with the need to obtain precise information to demonstrate that efficiency. It is concerned with controlling what is taught in schools and making teachers generally more accountable for their work in the classroom. (ibid.)

Chitty goes on to describe more specific differences between those two models. Whereas the professional approach emphasizes the quality of input and the skills, knowledge and awareness of the teacher, the bureaucratic approach concentrates on output and testing. The professional approach is based on individual differences and the learning process, but the bureaucratic approach is associated with norms and bench marks, norm-related criteria and judgements based on the expectations of how a statistically-normal child should perform. Attainment targets have the bureaucratic advantage of the presentation of statistics that allow comparison between teachers and schools. Finally, he argues that the professional curriculum is concerned with areas of learning and experience, while the bureaucratic curriculum is preoccupied with traditional subject boundaries.

But is any of this likely to have any effect on primary schools? Evidence suggests that even the Plowden report was not as significant as influence on primary schools as many critics of primary education would have us believe (Simon, 1980). Yet, the impending National Curriculum *is* likely to be significantly more influential, and has raised many concerns in primary quarters, particularly in relation to the narrowing of the curriculum, the increasing emphasis to be placed on testing and assessment, and the potential alienation of children. As has been explained, this chapter proposes to focus upon the implications of the Education Act for practice in primary schools — particularly in relation to proposals for assessment. Clearly, what I have to say has to be seen as tentative, even speculative; but as far as possible it will be based upon evidence derived from the work of those currently addressing the issues involved.

Assessment and the National Curriculum

As Broadfoot has recently argued (1988), a major feature of the increasing bureaucratization of education is the centrality of assessment in Government proposals.

The Consultation document emphasized this, by including assessments at 7, 11, 14 and 16, the purposes of which will be to assess the extent to which children have reached attainment targets in the core subjects of English, maths, science, and seven other foundation subjects. The main purpose of such assessment will be to show what a pupil has learnt and mastered and to enable teachers and parents to ensure that adequate progress is being achieved. Much of the assessment at 7, 11, 14 and at 16 (for non-examined subjects) will be done by teachers as part of normal classroom work.

> But at the heart of the assessment process there will be nationally prescribed tests done by all pupils to supplement the individual teachers' assessment. Teachers will administer and mark these, but their marking — and their assessments overall — will be externally moderated. (DES, 1987: par. 29)

More recently, in the Supplementary papers of the Task Group on Assessment and Testing (DES, 1988) we are informed that, in the moderation process, teachers' assessments would need to conform to patterns that emerge from the analysis of pupils' performances on the nationally prescribed tests, which implies a devaluing of teachers' assessments. This has been confirmed to some extent by the proposals from SEAC described in the previous chapter.

All of this confirms Broadfoot's (1988) view that at the centre of the Government's proposals lie the assumptions that, '. . . standards can be raised by the pervasive influence of comparison and competition,' and that 'accountability will lead to increased efficiency and hence productivity in education.' All of which, of course, is untested at present.

General Reactions to National Testing

Wholesale national testing is not without its critics, however. David Hopkins has offered four main concerns about the Government's proposals. Firstly, he believes that national testing will inevitably lead to divisiveness in schools. A national testing system, of necessity, separates pupils into high and low achievers and creates a system which confronts children with failure at regular intervals during their school lives.

The Task Group report (DES, 1987) has attempted to remedy this by an emphasis on criterion-referenced assessment, the benefits of which were discussed earlier. Not all educationists accept the supposed benefits of criterion-referenced assessment. Mary Simpson, drawing on the more extensive Scottish experience of criterion-referenced assessment, has argued:

> In terms of the use and practice of assessment,
> . . . Teachers found the assessment to be extremely time-consuming.
> . . . Teachers found the assessment merely told them, in greater detail than they believed necessary, what they already knew.
> . . . It pointed to no new kind of remedial action. (Simpson, 1990)

Instead, she argued for assessment strategies to allow pupils' actual knowledge to influence their learning: a point endorsed by recent research (Driver, 1988; Harlen and Black, 1989; Mercer and Edwards, 1987).

It is also the case that the assessments that emerge are then subject to moderation which implies norm-referencing, where (it is expected) children will be compared with their peers in the immediate locality. The results for an individual school are also likely to be subject to comparison with schools nationally, a further factor that could lead to normative comparison and the setting up of expectations of typical results.

The second criticism offered by Hopkins is that national testing trivializes the nature of knowledge, and might lead teachers to teach to the tests, which by implication would lead to a narrowing of the curriculum and reduction in its overall breadth and balance.

> Introducing a high-profile national system of standardized testing linked to a national curriculum is tantamount to making a public statement to the effect that a pupil's education is successful to the extent that he or she scores well on a range of narrowly defined tests. (Hopkins, 1988)

If this is all that is valued in education it is a narrow and impoverished view, and certainly contradicts the aims and intentions of many primary teachers.

In this context, Simons has commented

... 'breadth and balance', so regularly intoned by ministers in justification of the foundation curriculum ... is ... fatally undermined by subjection to conventional achievement tests, which depend upon narrowly stipulative domains of learning. (Simons, 1988)

It is already the case that a hierarchy is emerging within the National Curriculum. Given the increasing concern about the excessive burden that assessment is likely to place upon teachers, especially in the primary school, the most recent pronouncement from the present Secretary of State, John MacGregor, is that National Assessment by Standardized Tasks at 7 and probably at 11 will focus upon the core subjects of maths, science and English. Final decisions about national assessment of the foundation subjects history and geography at age 11 will await publication of the Work Group final reports. The Secretary of State has also invited the Schools Examination and Assessment Council (SEAC) to produce some non-statutory assessment tasks

> ... he has proposed that for technology, history and geography the statutory assessments should be carried out by teachers, supported by SATs but not used on a compulsory basis. He has asked SEAC to advise him whether effective, consistent and reliable assessments by teachers can be achieved nationally in this way. (*SEAC Recorder No. 5*, 1990)

The remaining Foundation subjects of PE, music and art will be provided with notes of guidance, which by implication are unlikely to contain assessment advice.

Hartnett and Naish suggest that, as a result, state schools will be franchised to deliver the National Curriculum, which they describe as the equivalent of fast food.

> For franchised schools the big burger will be the core subjects of English, maths and science. The foundation subjects will increasingly be seen as the squirt on the top ... For those who can afford it the cuisine proper will be available in the private sector, where the teachers, unencumbered by bureaucrats, will be able to concentrate on producing real food. (Hartnett and Naish, 1990: 14)

With regard to Hopkins' suggestion that the production of Standard Assessment Tasks will lead to teaching to the tests, there is still some hope that this may not be the case. Despite the heavy assessment demands the trials made upon teachers, those involved in them have recognized the contribution the experience is making to their increased understanding of their children and of the learning process. One teacher commented recently, after participating in some of the trial training, that the children in her class so enjoyed the experience, they asked if they could do more the following day! However, there is certainly evidence that, as presently organized, SATs are imposing an extremely demanding burden on teachers and will need to be modified before the first full assessments take place in 1991 (*TES*, 25 May 1990).[1]

A further issue of importance in the development of standardized tasks has been the suggestion that they should be differentiated. This has been interpreted in two different ways by the groups who are developing the tasks. One group has opted to differentiate by task: in other words, teachers will make the decision as to which tasks are most suitable for individual children, and offer a level-1 task to a level-1 child, level-2 task to a level-2 child, etc. The major difficulty of this proposal is an implicit labelling of the children, rather than allowing them to demonstrate what they are able to do, which is a basic principle of criterion-referenced assessment. There is the possibility, however, that if children demonstrate competence beyond the teacher's expectation they can be given a more demanding set of activities from the next level. The alternative to this view of differentiation that has been adopted by the other two development groups is to differentiate by outcome. This implies that teachers will be required to decide, on the basis of provided criteria, the level of performance of the children at the end of each task. The children will all engage in the same task, but the task will be organized so that a range of responses is possible.

It is important to recognize, however, that differentiation can occur in many other ways. Andrew Pollard suggests that, if assessment is to be equitable, we need to ask

> ...whether there are patterns of differentiation which might represent a less than just and fair treatment of the individual attributes and rights of each child and each social group. (Pollard, 1987)

In our assessments both within the classroom and through SATs, therefore, we need to reflect on differentiation as it occurs:

in the content and form of the curriculum;
in the ways in which the classroom is managed;
in the use of language;
in the expectations we have of each of our children;
in the ways in which we value and reinforce particular behaviours.

All of these have implications for particular groups of children of different social class origins, for those from different ethnic backgrounds, and for those with special educational needs. The *Times Educational Supplement* (22 June 1990) reported on the concerns expressed about the implications of standard assessment for bilingual children. A 7-year-old whose first language was Punjabi could not be fairly tested alongside a child whose first language was English, it was argued. Community languages such as Punjabi were in danger of being regarded as of low status in such a context.

Ruth Sutton offers another view of differentiation:

> Some teachers find this idea baffling, but it's pretty basic really. It means you need to take account of the different ways in which children learn and what their starting points are . . . what you need to do is to use as wide a range of teaching styles as you can manage to ensure that you cover the preferred ways of learning of different children. That doesn't mean never teach from the front, but don't do it all the time. Different attainment targets lend themselves to different teaching and learning methods, and you still have control of *how* you teach, even if the National Curriculum lays down some (not all) of *what* you teach. (Sutton, 1990: 21)

A third criticism offered by Hopkins of national testing is that it neglects the process of education. Current research on the effectiveness of schools emphasizes teacher professionalism, where collegiality, shared decision-making, and school based in-service is central, not a role for teachers as transmitters of a nationally-prescribed curriculum content. This is an issue commented upon recently by Helen Simons:

> In the plethora of critique that has accompanied the National Curriculum consultation document, relatively little attention has been paid to the professional role of the teacher and the loss to our education system of the pedagogical and curriculum developments that have taken place over the past twenty-five years. . . .
>
> The implication . . . is that there will be no room for curriculum development other than that related to the National Curriculum, and only then by schools chosen by the Secretary of State. . . . testing and schemes of work will confine pedagogy to what is conducive to publicly comparable performance, and the responsibility for curriculum experimentation, development, growth and change — the hallmark of educational professionalism — will no longer be the concern of teachers, schools or localities. They are destined to become the implementers of curricula, judged nevertheless by the success of treatments they no longer devise. (Simons, 1988)

Finally, Hopkins believes that there is evidence that systems of national testing just do not work. He describes a recent study in the United States which suggests that standardized teaching and learning result in short-term increases in test scores at the expense of boredom and failure. A four-year research project on the Madeleine Hunter 'Follow-through programme' in California reports short-term positive effects but no lasting changes: in fact, there were decreases in student scores in the final year of the programme. The researchers involved concluded that such assessment-led approaches to teaching and learning could not sustain teacher or pupil interest, and teaching in this way restricted the generation and exchange of ideas. Whilst establishing proposals for the National Curriculum, Kenneth Baker argued, however, that he recognized the inhibiting influences of a national curriculum and the potential reduction of innovation, and believed that these limitations could be avoided

> . . . by designing the system so as to encourage flexibility. I intend to ensure that schools will be perfectly free to adapt their teaching to new opportunities as they become available. (*Times Educational Supplement*, 25 September 1987)

Reactions from the Primary Sector

With regard to assessment and testing in primary schools, critics of the current state of primary education are to be found in the higher echelons of Her Majesty's Inspectorate, as the comment cited earlier by Eric Bolton, the Chief HMI, suggests:

> We lack broad agreement about how to describe and scrutinize the primary curriculum. The absence of clarity and agreement about what children should be capable of at various stages of their primary education leads to a distinct lack of information about standards of pupil achievement in individual primary schools and a consequent difficulty of establishing any standards of achievement as a basis for an assessment of performance. (Bolton, 1986)

This was closely followed in October 1986 by Kenneth Baker's saying he wanted to establish attainment targets for children of different ages because a child's full potential can be developed only if his or her progress is fairly and reliably assessed at stages along the way.

Criticisms of this view have been vehement in primary circles. David McNamara, for example, has argued that:

However strong the educational or political case for a national curriculum, it has little chance of being well taught by committed teachers unless ministers and the DES can provide coming generations of beginning teachers with some vision of primary education for adult society. Primary teaching and working with young children must be seen as rewarding and exciting activities in their own right. (*TES*, 28 October 1988)

Michael Armstrong, a strong advocate of child-centred primary practice, also presents some forcible critical views. Tests, he argues, whether of the more formal pencil-and-paper variety preferred by Mrs Thatcher, or of the kind advocated in the Task Group Report on Assessment and Testing, '. . . measure no more than the *shadow* of achievement.' (Armstrong, 1988)

The role of tests, he suggests, is peripheral to assessment. He admits that sometimes they help in the diagnosis of weaknesses, the identification of gaps in knowledge and understanding, and provide an indication of unevenness in development. They can also be used to demonstrate children's competence in a limited range of specific tasks.

> But when the shadow is mistaken for the substance — when nationally prescribed tests are placed at the *centre* of a school's assessment of its pupils and become the chief criterion of comparison between children, teachers and schools — then children's individual accomplishments will at best be caricatured and at worst be altogether denied. (ibid.)

To describe children's achievements adequately, Armstrong believes we require 'a critical account of their most significant pursuits':

> of their stories, their paintings, their scientific investigations, their mathematical speculations, their historical researches, and especially of the work on which they have lavished the greatest care and enthusiasm. (ibid.)

To offer a detailed critical analysis of this kind requires professional commitment, developed observational skill, reflection, and knowledge of the child whose achievement is being considered.

> In the end individual achievement is incommensurable. The act of measurement is inevitably an act of reduction and rejection — an act which deprives many children of the value of their own accomplishments. (ibid.)

Caroline Gipps (1983, 1987) reminds us, however, that a great deal of testing already goes on in primary schools. In two surveys undertaken to investigate the extent of testing routinely undertaken with all or any part of the primary age group, Gipps and her colleagues found a considerable range of testing already in existence, at the ages of 7, 8 and 11 in particular. If this is the case, why are the new proposals so threatening? In a more recent article (1988), Gipps suggests that there are three ways in which the new proposals are different from the existing use of tests. The tests currently most in use are standardized group tests for reading, reasoning and mathematics, not specifically related to the curriculum. In the new proposals, testing, as we have seen, is central to the National Curriculum; its purpose is to see that the curriculum is being properly taught. Results from tests currently used have often been part of the process of identification of children with special educational needs, or have been made available to the next teacher or school, or to local authorities in their monitoring of standards, which Gipps believed was of limited significance. Under the new proposals, Gipps suggests that children are likely to be classified much more formally than in the past, right from the start of their junior education. Also, because results have to be made public, teachers will feel under pressure to get good results. The final concern she expresses is about the very nature of the tasks which, as has been suggested, are expected to be 'differentiated', meaning that the children will be classified according to how they perform. At present children can complete their primary education without a sense of failure, but 'Under the new examining system . . . there is a return to competitiveness and an emphasis on individual effort . . . encouraged as part of a plan for economic recovery'.

This leads Gipps to the rather depressing view that

> . . . the disadvantages associated with the proposed system of national assessment at primary level outweigh the possible positive impact. Primary schools under the new arrangements will be a good deal more like secondary schools in being under the influence of exam board constraints (who have the responsibility for moderation). More ability banding, more competition, formal teaching relationships and methods, stricter subject boundaries . . . (Gipps, 1988)

Such concerns were succinctly discussed in an article written by a teacher of 5–7 year olds who described her concern about testing four individual children from her class. Shane usually goes to school only four days a week, because noisy upstairs neighbours prevent him sleeping at night, so he sometimes goes to his Nan's so he can sleep there. Kelly also works a three- or four-day week, because she visits her Dad who has recently moved out. Katrina is covered in a nasty rash, her mother rarely sending her to school. Paul has been waiting for something to be done about his hearing. He tries hard, and is thought to be quite bright, but will go to the juniors a virtual non-reader because it is not easy being in a primary classroom if your hearing is poor. She concludes,

> I would not mind an inspector questioning me on the way I teach reading. I would not mind people who knew what they were talking about testing the children in my class and offering criticism and advice. All I would like to be sure of is that those who assess my children's reading ability and, by implication, my teaching, and those who judge the school from these results, will know and understand about Paul's hearing, Shane's neighbour, Kelly's absence, and Katrina's blessed forgetfulness. Unfortunately, I don't think they will. (*Independent*, 13 April 1989)

Where Do We Go From Here?

It was with bated breath that most primary school teachers awaited the advice of the Schools Examination and Assessment Council on classroom assessment. This appeared in the form of three glossy documents in January 1990. Reactions have tended to be of amazement at the complexity proposed, and the opinion that they are of limited help to the primary teachers struggling to organize an assessment strategy in their classrooms. The SEAC advice seems to assume that primary teachers do little else than assess. Gipps commented:

> The packs focus on assessment at the level of statements of attainment and the message is that every statement of attainment has to be assessed. Unfortunately the sums do not work. Even if teachers start small and do five statements of attainment a day or three statements of attainment on three children per day (as the packs suggest) they still cannot cover the 200–300 statements per child. The model is too complex and must be simplified. (Gipps, 1990)

The SEAC documents offer the mnemonic, INFORM, to help structure the process of assessment. Ted Wragg offers an alternative:

SEAC	WRAGG
Identify the S of A your lesson will promote	Is this monumental bullshit really necessary?
Note carefully opportunities for children to demonstrate achievement	No one who applies it to the letter will remain sane
Focus upon the performance, looking for evidence of achievement	For goodness sake, throw it in the bin and start again
Offer the child a chance to discuss what the activity was for and what was achieved	Only twenty-five hours a day will be needed
Record what you have identified as noteworthy	Radically reduce the bureaucracy
Modify your teaching plan for the child, if necessary, to manage the next stage of learning	More teachers will quit the profession if you don't

(*Times Educational Supplement*, 10 Feb. 1990)

In response to such criticism, Christie comments that fair assessment requires agreed criteria of progression and that statements of attainment are a first attempt. These will need to be refined in the light of experience. The SEAC guide requires teachers to find half an hour of 'undivided attention' for each child every term, which he believes is not unreasonable:

> The guide suggests that this time be distributed as five minutes work with the child once a fortnight, focused on a genuine classroom activity and allowing feedback on three or four facets of the child's work. At this rate, the progress of every child in the class can be explored in every one of the 39 current attainment targets about once every two terms — that is, three times during the expected period of transition from one level of any attainment target to another. Whether, or how, this work is recorded is for the teacher to decide. As the guide stresses, it is the steps teacher and child take as a result of assessment that will make a difference. And a difference is needed. The demotivating effects of norm-referenced testing as the major course of educational feedback are plain for all to see. (Christie, 1990)

The SEAC advice has led to a proliferation of checklists and proformas in primary schools, the purpose of which is to gather together evidence on children's achievements in relation to the statements of attainment. The Secretary of State is reported to have said that teachers have 'jumped the gun' on assessment (*TES*, 9 March 1990), and that on his visits to primary schools he 'has been assailed by teachers waving elaborate matrices containing 70 boxes to be filled in for each seven-year-old'. The demands that this is making upon teachers have been commented upon by Her

Majesty's Senior Chief Inspector of Schools who suggests that excessive assessment may undermine teachers' job satisfaction and morale. He commented:

> If actually carrying out assessments, recording and reporting outcomes and accounting for what has been done do turn out to be overly prescriptive and inquisitorial, not only will the quality of teaching and learning be adversely affected, but the competence, professionalism and creativity of the teaching force may be undermined. (DES, 1990: par. 25)

There still appears to be uncertainty about how and what to record. Does the provision of an experience actually imply achievement? Does 'understanding now mean that it is retained'? The Scottish Council for Research in Education recently produced a publication describing assessment practice in primary schools in Scotland. They drew a distinction between children as having been *introduced* to something, having *understood* something and having *internalized* a particular piece of learning, but recognized the potential complexity of making judgements in relation to each of these categories:

> The teacher knows when some aspect of mathematics has been introduced to a particular child, and recording this information is useful for avoiding gaps in development. However, the other two code descriptions depend on observation of each child's behaviour. The teachers have to look for evidence of understanding or internalization in what the children are doing. What kind of evidence is acceptable? What observable difference is there between understanding and internalization? The fact that teachers clearly believe there is an important difference is indicated by some of our sample survey schools sending us similar methods of recording as part of their schools' assessment policy, 'developing, assimilated, established' or 'has been taught, capable of, mastery of'. Considerable debate must take place amongst staff if these phrases are to be interpreted with any degree of consistency. (Black *et al.*, 1989: 31)

This degree of consistency can only be achieved by recognizing the complexity of learning and by involving teachers in the process of reflecting upon that judgement.

One Step Forward?

With such a depressing scenario, are there any advantages to be gained? I would like to think that there are. As we have seen, one central feature of the Task Group proposals is the emphasis upon *formative* assessment, which means that the results of any of the testing will provide information to the teacher which should influence the organization and structure of future learning both for individual children and the class as a whole. A second important element of the proposals is that assessment should be concerned with finding out *what children know and can do*.

Once the proposals are established and modified so that they are workable, it is likely that assessment will be more systematic. Criteria for judgements will be clearer and more explicit, which will contribute towards improved justification of our practice. This, alongside a common language which teachers and parents will grow to understand, should improve parent–school communication and, by implication, contribute towards improving parent–school relationships.

It is also the case that a fundamental role for teachers is envisaged, both in terms of undertaking assessments and feeding this back into the progressive development of the National Curriculum. The next chapter begins to explore what this might involve.

Note

1. In the summer of 1990 SATs were trialled in a 2% sample of schools throughout the country. The evaluations of this experience suggest that all the SATs tried to assess too much, took too much teaching time and demanded too much of teachers' goodwill. The major recommendation to have emerged is that during the first full unreported run during the summer term of 1991, SATs must focus on fewer statements of attainment, take up less teaching time and be more manageable in the classroom.

Chapter 4

Strategies for Assessment: Observation

> Lasting Change in Education comes not from central advisers and
> researchers handing down pre-packaged innovations, but from
> individual pioneers modifying their classroom practice in response
> to *observation* of their own pupils. (Christian Schiller)

The process of observation is going to be one of the major ways in which
teachers will gather together the evidence upon which to base their
judgements about children's progress in the National Curriculum, and by
implication is an important means by which we will assess children's
achievements. As has been suggested earlier, however, it is important to
recognize that such observation is not an additional expectation of teachers,
but draws upon skills already in use in the day-to-day activity of most
primary classrooms. What is going to be required, however, is a clearer
understanding and more explicitly expressed idea of the strengths and
weaknesses of observational procedures and the information which is
elicited. We need to develop and extend our skills of observation, to go
beyond looking to seeing, and I would argue that not only do we learn more
about children and their learning by improved observation, but we also learn
more about the learning process itself and the extent of our involvement in
supporting or preventing learning from taking place. The importance of
observation was recognized by the Task Group when they commented that:

> Teachers make frequent judgements about children's performance
> to decide whether they are ready to go on to new work. Sometimes
> the decision can be settled quickly; at other times *much detailed
> observation* is needed so that a teacher can be sure, or can discover
> more precisely what is restricting progress. (DES. 1988 TGAT: A
> Digest)

This chapter will offer an overview of issues associated with observation and assessment, and suggest ways in which teacher observation might be improved and extended. The issued to be addressed are that:

observation is a natural process;
observation is a central teaching skill;
observation is more than looking;
observation should be purposeful;
whether all see the same things;
the more you look, the more you see.

Observation is a Natural Process

It is important to remember that reflecting upon and refining one's observational skills focus upon abilities that are a natural human resource. Observation is central to our understanding of people generally and is often undertaken intuitively, perhaps without realizing it. Derek Rowntree addresses this when he asks:

How do we come to know other persons (or they us)? Through what means do we come to hold beliefs about them which we take to be justified? Often we learn about them without really trying. In the course of our everyday interactions with them we form impressions, tentative at first perhaps, which subsequent experience of them either increasingly confirms, complicates, or else negates. Our everyday assessments of other people come mostly through observation of, and reflection on, events and episodes that arise in the course of living, working and playing together. (Rowntree, 1977)

Much as I would agree with the sentiments expressed here, the one comment I would take issue with concerns *reflection*. As Jane Abercrombie (1969) reminds us, rarely do we carefully reflect upon our initial judgements, which are embedded in our own personality. This is not surprising, given the extensive nature of our daily interactions, especially in the primary classroom. Martyn Long summarizes this when he comments:

The taken-for-granted is our experience as it is lived largely unreflectively. The very words 'taken for granted' imply that our lived experience is constituted of situations and events that we do not question or probe. We lower our consciousness, often deliberately, to avoid the pain of reflecting or acting more thoughtfully. Lest this sound too perjorative, it is an entirely necessary ploy to reduce the complexity of life. (Long, 1989)

The demands of observation for assessment purposes will require us to learn to question our judgements, to act reflectively and to take comment from others as information to help us to make more reliable judgements, rather than to take it as personal criticism. Joan Dean recognizes this when she suggests:

> Normal living involves us all in the process of making judgements about people and events in order to predict what may happen and decide what to do next. We do this from a very early age and it becomes our normal response to new situations. This is evident when you go to a course or if you are on holiday and meet new people. You listen to them, look at them and ask questions to discover the ways in which they are like you and the ways in which they differ and what their interests are and so on. The judgements you make may not always be accurate, but this may not matter in such circumstances, particularly if you are aware that you are making judgements on inadequate evidence.
>
> As a professional teacher, however, you need to be much more sure of your evidence because much depends upon the outcome of your judgements. You therefore need to extend the everyday practice of making judgements in order to make sure that judgements you make are as valid as possible. (Dean, 1990)

Observation is a Central Teaching Skill

During our everyday interactions with colleagues and children we are continually looking, seeing and interpreting. The processes involved and their importance at the classroom level were commented upon in the Parliamentary Select Committee Report:

> The greater proportion of judgements made by a teacher must be made subjectively in the sense that they must be reached quickly without going systematically through a series of criteria and externally determined references. Their quality depends on close observation and the capacity to apply a breadth of experience and, in its broadest sense, training. The fact that these judgements are vital to children's progress and inescapable suggests that much of initial and inservice training should be directed at helping teachers to make them effectively. (HMSO, 1986: par. 7.24)

There are two factors which need to be addressed in relation to these comments and they concern *breadth of experience* and *training*. As far as breadth of experience is concerned, it is very easy for us to assume that our experience provides us with a broad means of comparing the achievements of our children and judging them appropriately. The TGAT report commented:

> We are all, as individuals, persuaded that those things that occur frequently in our experience are normal. Schools' catchment areas are not representative of the national population, but they condition teachers' expectations of what is 'normal'.
>
> These expectations are powerfully reinforced by successive year groups of pupils. In the absence of equally powerful external evidence, teachers' expectations become the teachers' 'standards'. (DES, 1988: par. 65)

As far as training is concerned, it is often the case, however, that many of us have had limited experience associated with developing our skills of observation and reflecting on judgements derived from such observations. One of the pioneers who advocated using observations of children in real situations was Jean Piaget, who, though much criticized in recent years, has contributed considerably to our understanding of children's intellectual development. Piaget developed his 'clinical method' as a way of exploring the development of children's understanding, and employed observation along with interview as a means of accessing children's views of the world. This takes us to the next issue in observation: that it is more than just looking.

Observation is More Than Just Looking

Wynne Harlen, Professor of Science Education at the University of Liverpool and a member of the National Curriculum Science Working Party, was significantly influenced by the ideas of Jean Piaget. This influence is seen especially in her work on Science 5–13, a Schools Council Project developed in the 1970s, but also in her work on the Progress in Learning Science Course, published under the title of *Match and Mismatch*. In this project, one question asked about progress in learning science was, what can we do instead of testing to monitor children's progress? Their response was to draw upon the observations that teachers are making all the time of children's actions, responses and behaviours of different kinds.

> Children are showing their attitudes and abilities all the time in their normal work; they are telling us all we need to know about their characteristics if only we can receive and interpret their messages. (Harlen, 1977)

Harlen argued strongly that this involved no more than many teachers were already doing, but, like Piaget, saw observation as involving more than just looking. Observation that serves a useful assessment purpose involves:

— *looking* at the way pupils go about their work and not just at the products: i.e., an emphasis on the processes of learning;
— *listening* to pupils' ideas and trying to understand their reasoning;
— *discussing* problems so that pupils reveal their ways of thinking.

As Peter Woods has suggested, the observer requires, 'a sharp eye, a keen ear and a sound memory'. (Woods, 1986)

Such observation provides a ready-made method for gathering information, which has the advantages that:

it is flexible and can be used at any time;
it does not interfere with normal activities or take up time;
it can provide information about behaviours of all kinds;
it can be used repeatedly, giving constant feedback;
children are unaware of the process;
it does not require special equipment or materials.

Teachers' reactions to such proposals, when I have shared the *Match and Mismatch* materials with them, have often been of the following kinds:

'How can I find the time to do this?'
'It's too time-consuming. It's not worth the effort.'
'My classroom is far too busy for this.'
'My children are too young; they need my help too often for me to be able to do it.'

Harlen has recognized the difficulties herself:

Whilst all teachers would feel that they observe children all the time, it must be appreciated that in a busy classroom, time to stop and observe in depth is limited.

Many classroom observations would be better likened to brief glimpses of a passing scene, and anyone who has attempted classroom observation will be sure that even in ideal conditions it is difficult to observe and interpret every action. (Harlen, 1977)

Despite this, it is still worth the effort, as many teachers will testify. One solution, which originated from the Open University Course, 'The Curriculum in Action', and has been used to good effect in a wide variety of contexts, is described as 'the Red Folder' (Essex Assessment Pack, 1989). What is suggested is that opportunities for observation should be negotiated with the children themselves, simply by explaining that you wish to look at what the children are doing, and carrying the red folder is an indication that observation is taking place. Teachers I have worked with have tried this and often, to their surprise, have found it worked most successfully. They initially observe for a short time and eventually build this up to more extensive and sustained observational periods. One teacher commented:

> I was amazed; I expected them to need my attention. I did as you suggested and said to my class (of five-year-olds), if they needed help while I was observing they could either ask someone on their table, or wait for me to put my folder down. I started with a couple of minutes on each child and now I am able to concentrate for quite long periods. The fascinating thing is I've begun to see things that I never noticed before. (Personal comment on reflections on an Observation Course)

A useful explanation of the procedure and the responses of the children can be seen in this commentary from the Essex In-service pack on Assessment and Testing:

> This is a very effective way of observing the children in your class while at the same time allowing the recording of those observations without the presence of additional supporting staff.

Below is an example of how this was tried by a lower junior teacher:

> On the first day that I experimented with this technique, I gathered together my class of lower juniors and explained that, as part of my job as a teacher, from time to time it was necessary for me to stop and look at what they were actually doing and sometimes to write things down. I emphasized that I was looking at all sorts of different things and that sometimes I might be looking at the way a group were working together or sometimes at one or two individual children. I stressed that it was to help me and not to find fault with them.
>
> I continued to explain that I would be using a special *red folder* and that if they saw me with my folder in my hands then they were to go away and not to disturb me. As soon as I put my folder down they could return to talk to me. I said that it would only happen once or twice a week, but that I would always tell them beforehand.
>
> The children responded magnificently because they really felt they were helping me, and my first session was spent in writing down whatever came to mind as I spent most of that occasion testing their reactions and listening to their comments:

'Look, she's got her folder, sit down.'
'No, go away, we mustn't.'
'Let's get on with ——until we can ask her.'
'Please Miss can I go to the toilet?'

Yes, of course it wasn't 100% response but . . . as I repeated the sessions they all began to realize that as I would totally ignore them anyway there wasn't a lot of point asking while I was using my folder and that it could wait until I was free. Now the children are used to my activity they respond extremely well, enabling me to carry out some very worthwhile observations within my classroom (now without the need for the folder).

I found the children needed to be settled in activities that they were able to work at reasonably independently.

The Essex group have produced a videotape of this activity for use in in-service sessions, and the notes accompanying this material offer further advice for others proposing to adopt this procedure. They have framed a series of pertinent suggestions for preparation for observations of this kind:

Prepare for your observation; consider all possible interruptions and attempt to divert them.

Prepare your focus — one child, a group of children, the interaction between them, their social relations.

If the focus is one child, develop strategies to reduce their anxiety or ensure that he/she remains unaware that they are the focus of attention.

Prepare beforehand relevant background notes and record your observations carefully. You develop your own strategies for this.

These suggestions lead us on to the next major issue in observation: that observation should be purposeful. The teacher who described the experiences above commented that her early attempts at this procedure, undertaken without prior reflection, were not particularly successful:

The one time I tried it without planning beforehand, I found half an hour had passed without recording anything . . .

What you are actually looking for may depend on the particular child in mind, the activity, or the assessment purpose. This is a point identified by Christian Schiller when he suggested that:

The value of an observation depends on the judgements as well as the skill of the observer. To assess attainment it must be observed in the round. Such observation is not easy. The observer has not only to use keenly his eyes and ears, but to know where to direct them; he has not only to see and hear the shape of the event, but to perceive its quality. (Griffin-Beale, 1984)

Clearly, then, it is important that the observations undertaken should have a clearly identified purpose.

Observation Should Be Purposeful

Colin Hook suggested that:

Classroom observation is more than just sitting and watching. It is looking with a purpose, using techniques to record or encode what is observed. The ability to observe is not innate or inherited. It is developed systematically and progressively from simple beginnings, with the observation of one child, a specific behaviour, or a simple scene, to more elaborate settings with complex means of identifying and recording teacher and pupil behaviour. The observer role is one that should be in every teacher's repertoire, and the skills involved are part of his 'tools of the trade'. The ability to view classroom events analytically and critically is acquired through the recognition, recording, measurement and interpretation of naturally-occurring activities, and an understanding of the variety of perspectives possible in most situations. (Hook, 1985)

Strategies in observation can be described along a continuum from open, unstructured situations where there is no clear purpose (these often give an opportunity to frame some clear intention for later observation), to highly structured, systematic observation-procedures where clear and specific criteria are identified to base the observation upon. The diagram below attempts to capture the range, with examples to illustrate each of them.

Illustrations of Each of the Above Observational Procedures

Open–Non-specific

Many of the first attempts at classroom observation are of this kind, whether they be looking at your own classroom, at your own children, or visiting another school. It is an opportunity to look and see what is happening. Something may strike you as being of interest or of concern and lead you to

Figure 4.1: Kinds of Observation

Open – Non-specific
Non-judgemental
(Look, See, What
captures your attention?)

Focused Observation

(Looking at an individual child, or interactions between children in a group. Consideration of their 'on-task' activity or their language usage. Without particular categories to guide your attention.)

Systematic Observation

(Categories are identified beforehand and the observation often focuses upon timed sampling of a behaviour in terms of the prescribed categories.)

want to look again with more focus and on more occasions. The recent experiences of many teachers who had the opportunity to visit other schools through money released via GRIST (Grant Related In-service Training) or LEATGS (LEA Training Grants Schemes) have started with this kind of observation, as the following extract illustrates:

Mrs. A It was wonderful to be able to go and visit another school during the working day. It's the first chance I've had to do this since my training. I don't like to say how long ago that was!

C. C. Why did you visit that particular school?

Mrs. A Oh, no special reason. It serves a similar catchment area to ours and so it's interesting to see the similarities and differences. (data collected during an evaluation of a Local Authority GRIST scheme)

Another example of open observation comes from my own experience of trying to think of alternative arrangements of facilities in my classroom. I tried to look at the ways in which the children moved around the room, the ways they used facilities, what created difficulties for them and interrupted the flow of learning. I then made a scale diagram of the room and furniture, and together we considered possible alternative layouts, some of which we experimented with. I then focused on the effects of the changes we had proposed. In fact, I was able to involve the children in some of the observations. It provided them with plenty of information to sort, categorize and display with explanation to others.

Focused Observation

Examples have been offered above of the way in which open observation quickly becomes more focused and specifically purposeful. John Elliott, Professor of Education at the University of East Anglia, prefers this mode of observation. He advocates observation as an important strategy in classroom research, but believes any observation in classrooms, especially by an outside observer, should focus upon information of value to the teacher being observed. His major concern in observation of classrooms is to attempt to explain patterns of behaviour. He suggests that:

> To identify patterns, events that seem to recur time and time again would be important to attempt to explain. I'm not saying you go in as though your mind is a blank state; because you have experience and knowledge of classrooms you have a set of possible hypotheses . . . for investigation. (Elliott, 1983)

He goes on to suggest that:

> The point is to try to be open to new things . . . I don't think it matters that the children know I'm in the classroom. I think it's important that they're clear . . . about why I am there . . . to clarify why you're there and what you expect of them. (Elliott, 1983)

His idea of classroom research is where there is a sense in which the teacher and the children are in a very good position to know what's going on. . . . As an outside observer, he believes that he might be in a better position to notice certain things than the teacher and the pupils, who, after all, are involved in the action. So his view is that if the teacher and the pupils and an outside observer can pool together their knowledge and understanding of the situation, that is more likely to give a more comprehensive picture of what's going on. One is also quite likely to identify conflicts or differences in perspective and interpretation.

> So you've got a kind of 'triangulation' procedure where the pupils' understandings are elicited, the teacher's understandings are elicited, the outsider's understandings are elicited, and these are all fed back to the teacher. If classroom research is not useful, doesn't generate useful knowledge for the teacher, then it's valueless. (ibid.)

This applies to teachers' reflecting upon their own practice, as well as to situations where others are observing your practice.

Systematic Observation

Systematic observation procedures draw upon criteria that are carefully defined and highly specific, so that it is absolutely clear how the observations are to be undertaken and individual bias in perception be eradicated. They are often undertaken by trained observers. The typical characteristics of systematic observation have been described by Croll as follows:

1. It is explicit in its purpose or purposes, and the purposes have to be worked out before data collection is conducted.
2. It is explicit and rigorous in its definition of categories and in its criteria for classifying phenomena into these categories.
3. It produces data that can be presented in quantitative form and can be summarized and related to other data using statistical techniques.
4. Once the procedures for recording and criteria for using categories have been arrived at, the role of the observer is essentially one of following instructions to the letter, and any observer should record a particular event in an identical fashion to any other. (Croll, 1986)

Probably the most well-known systematic observational procedure is that developed by Ned Flanders, whose Interaction Category system focuses upon the language interaction in classrooms. It tends to be more appropriate for formal class lessons, but data derived from the development of the system led to the development of his 'Rule of two thirds'.

Two thirds of the time there is talk going on in classrooms, and two thirds of that talk is teacher talk. (Flanders, 1972)

Hopkins (1985) offers a succinct description of the procedure developed by Flanders. Details of each of the categories are presented in Figure 4.2.

Another example of systematic observation used in Great Britain comes from the Oracle Project based at the University of Leicester, coordinated by Maurice Galton. In this quantitative approach to observation the observer remains apart from the action. Galton admits:

It's very difficult for an outside observer simply to come in with no previous knowledge or experience of a classroom and sit at the back of the room and make decisions associated with a prescribed set of categories. It requires an observer to go in on a number of occasions and begin to identify the patterns that exist, the typical ways of working. As a result, you begin to understand the way in which the classroom works and the roles and responses of individual children.

Figure 4.2: Flanders' Interaction Analysis System

1. Every three seconds the observer writes down the category best describing the verbal behaviour of the teacher and class.

Teacher	1.	accepts feelings
talk	2.	praise
	3.	accepts ideas
	4.	question
	5.	lecture
	6.	command
	7.	criticism
Pupil	8.	solicited
talk	9.	unsolicited
	10.	silence

2. The numbers are written in sequence across the data sheet.
3. Each line of the data sheet contains twenty squares, thus representing approximately one minute of time.
4. Separate 'episodes' can be identified by scribbled margin notes, and a new line started for a new 'episode'.
5. In a research project the observer would have a pocket timer designed to give a signal every three seconds, thus reminding him or her to record a tally (a stop-watch or the secondhand of a wristwatch can be used).

(Flanders, 1972)

Figure 4.3a: The Observation Categories of the Teacher's Record in the Oracle Project

Conversation

Questions

Task
Q1   recalling facts
Q2   offering ideas, solutions (closed)   Marking
Q3   offering ideas, solutions (open)   Waiting
Task supervision
Q4   referring to task supervision
Routine
Q5   referring to routine matter

Statements
Task
S1   of facts
S2   of ideas, problems
Task supervision
S3   telling child what to do
S4   praising work or effort
S5   feedback on work or effort
Routine
S6   providing information, directions
S7   providing feedback
S8   of critical control
S9   of small talk

Silence

silent interaction

gesturing
showing

story
reading
not observed
not coded

no interaction
adult interaction
visiting pupil
not interacting
out of room

audience
composition
activity

Figure 4.3b: *The Observation Categories of the Pupil Record*

Category	Item	Brief definition of item
Coding the pupil-adult categories		
1 *Target's role*	INIT	Target attempts to become focus of attention (not focus at previous signal)
	STAR	Target is focus of attention
	PART	Target in audience (no child is focus)
	LSWT	Target in audience (another child is focus)
2 *Interacting adult*	TCHR	Target interacts with teacher
	OBSR	Target interacts with observer
	OTHER	Target ineracts with any other adult such as the head or secretary
3 *Adult's interaction*	TK WK	Adult interacts about task work (task content or supervision)
	ROUTINE	Adult interacts about routine matter (classroom management and control)
	POS	Adult reacts positively to task work (praises)
	NEG	Adult reacts negatively to behaviour etc. (criticizes)
	IGN	Adult ignores attempted initiation
4 *Adult's communication setting*	IND ATT	Adult gives private individual attention to target pupil
	GROUP	Adult gives private attention to target's group
	CLASS	Adult interacts with whole class
	OTHER	Adult gives private attention to another child or group or does not interact
Coding the pupil-pupil categories		
5 *Target's role*	BGNS	Target successfully begins a new contact
	COOP	Target cooperates by responding to an initiation
	TRIES	Target unsuccessfully tries to initiate
	IGN	Target ignores attempted initiation
	SUST	Target sustains interaction
6 *Mode of interaction*	MTL	Non-verbal, mediated solely by materials
	CNTC	Non-verbal, mediated by physical contact or gesture (with or without materials)
	VRB	Verbal (with or without materials, physical contact or gesture)
7a *Task of other pupil(s)*	S TK	Same as target's task
	D TK	Different from target's task
7b *Sex and number of other pupil(s)*	SS	Target interacts privately with one pupil of same sex
	OS	Target interacts privately with one pupil of opposite sex
	SEV SS	Target interacts publicly with two or more pupils having same sex as target
	SEV OS	Target interacts publicly with two or more pupils, of whom one at least is of the opposite sex to the target
7c *Base of other pupil(s)*	OWN BS	From target's own base
	OTH BS	From another base

Figure 4.3b: The Observation Categories of the Pupil Record (cont'd)

Category	Item	Brief definition of item
Coding the activity and location categories		
8 *Target's activity*	COOP TK	Fully involved and cooperating on approved task work (e.g. reading)
	COOP R	Fully involved and cooperating on approved routine work (e.g. sharpening a pencil)
	DSTR	Non-involved and totally distracted from all work
	DSTR OBSR	Non-involved and totally distracted from all work by the observer
	DSRP	Non-involved and aggressively disrupting work of other pupil(s)
	HPLY	Non-involved and engaging in horseplay with other pupil(s)
	WAIT TCHR	Waiting to interact with the teacher
	CODS	Partially cooperating and partially distracted from approved work
	INT TCHR	Interested in teacher's activity or private interaction with other pupil(s)
	INT PUP	Interested in the work of other pupil(s)
	WOA	Working on an alternative activity which is not approved work
	RIS	Not coded because the target is responding to internal stimuli
	NOT OBS	Not coded beause the target is not observed for some reason
	NOT LISTED	Not coded because the target's activity is not listed
9 *Target's location*	P IN	Target in base
	P OUT	Target out of base but not mobile
	P MOB	Target out of base and mobile
	P OUT RM	Target out of room
10 *Teacher activity and location*	T PRES	Teacher present with target through interaction or physical proximity
	T ELSE	Teacher privately interacting elsewhere with other pupil(s) or visitor
	T MNTR	Teacher not interacting but monitoring classroom activities
	T HSKP	Teacher not interacting but housekeeping
	T OUT RM	Teacher out of room

The target pupil's behaviour was coded at regular twenty-five second intervals using a method of multiple coding

The Oracle project used two main instruments, the 'Pupil record' and the 'Teacher record', details of which are given in Figure 4.3a and 4.3b.

The Pupil record was developed from an American Instrument, PROSE (the Personal Record of School Experience), which was modified to take into account features typical of the primary classroom in Great Britain. The categories have arisen from general discussion and expectations of many people about what goes on in classrooms. The roots of such observational procedures are often traced to the seminal work of Flanders.

A useful critique of systematic observation procedures can be found in a recent publication by Graham Hitchcock and David Hughes (Hitchcock and Hughes, 1989, pp. 139–143).

An example of what systematic observation might mean in practice for teachers is based upon the opportunity one class teacher had to spend time in another colleague's classroom. The observer, who was on an in-service course, was invited to spend one day a week in someone else's classroom observing. The visitor was to negotiate with the class teacher what the observation should focus upon, so that both the observer and the observed gained from the experience. In the example described, the teacher wanted the observer to focus particularly on two children, Jane and Nicholas, for specific reasons. Jane was extremely quiet and Nicholas was often in trouble. The observer spent the first day keeping detailed notes about each activity that the children were involved in throughout the day, including the time spent on the activity. The observer then went away and tried to describe the day in terms of the different experiences of the children. The picture that emerged is presented in Figure 4.4.

Further reflection upon this information raises many interesting questions about the children's day.

Nicholas spent more time on musical activity — why?

Nicholas spent less time listening to the teacher — why?

Both children spent considerable time queueing — why?

The amount of time for each child individually with the teacher was extremely limited. What can the teacher do about it?

It was also the case that there were significant differences in the kind of interaction between the teacher and the two children. Jane's two minutes was made up of two interactions and Nicholas's of over 20, many of which were negative. This led to a series of exercises to develop and improve the learning experiences of the children involved, with the observer playing a very important part in the process.

Figure 4.4: An Example of an Observational Analysis

	Jane	Nicholas
Breaks and movement	1 hr 28 mins	1 hr 27 mins
Musical activity and rehearsal	1 hr 27 mins	2 hrs 05 mins
Listening to teacher and general discussion	35 mins	19 mins
Queuing	19 mins	28 mins
Mathematics	16 mins	25 mins
Handwriting	10 mins	3 mins
Reading/workshop cards	22 mins	6 mins
Talking individually to the teacher	2 mins	4 mins

Information from activities such as these reveals important information for the teacher about his or her classroom. It can also provide information to serve assessment purposes if the right kind of questions are asked.

Structuring and Recording Observations

One further important feature that emerges from a consideration of *kinds of observation* concerns the means by which we can most effectively structure, note and record our observations. As far as structuring is concerned, I have always found the following questions a useful organizational tool to prepare myself for the process:

What is the purpose of the observation?
Who will be involved?
Where is the observation to take place?
When is the observation to take place?
Why? Am I clear about the purpose?
How? Have I thought about the most effective procedure to suit the stated purpose?

Recording observations is dependent upon the procedure adopted. If a systematic procedure is employed it often produces tick-lists which are calculated as percentages of time, whereas focused and open-ended techniques usually require some kind of note-taking procedure that the observer develops and improves over time. An excellent illustration of how such a system can be built up and modified through use comes from the study in *Child Watching at Playgroup and Nursery School* by Sylva *et al.* (1980), a copy of which is included as Appendix A.

Each of the observational procedures described are subject to the bias, prejudice and value-judgement of the observer. Even in systematic observation, where there is an attempt to achieve rigour and objectivity, it is recognized that the researcher/observer's opinion may not be that of others (Croll, 1986). This moves us to the next important issue in observation: do we all see the same things?

Do We All See the Same Things?

The whole issues of perception, interpretation and judgement are central features of the assessment process, and we have to recognize that we never undertake observation in a vacuum. As Jane Abercrombie has suggested:

... what is being perceived depends not only on what is being looked at but on the state of the perceiver. (Abercrombie, 1969: 27)

We tend to think of ourselves as passively receiving information from the outside world, but this is far from the case; in the process of receiving information we interpret and judge. (ibid.: 29)

When the thing we look at is sufficiently like the thing we expect to see, and easily fits our scheme, our experience helps us to see. It is only when what we expect to see is not there that our schemata lead us astray. (ibid.: 33)

We never come to an act of perception with an entirely blank mind, but are always in a state of preparedness or expectancy, because of our past experience. (ibid.: 63)

Concern about the potential problems of bias in our observations and assessment expectations has been commented upon by the Task Group on Assessment and Testing.

Teachers' expectations of individual pupils in the classroom can create problems, loosely referred to as 'the Halo effect'. In the absence of a close definition of what to look for and how to observe it, we look for confirmation of our expectations. Research evidence shows that teachers' rank orders of pupils' performance may vary systematically from rank orders produced by tests users. (DES, 1988: par. 66)

The moderation procedures, which were described earlier in Chapter 2, are offered as a means of overcoming some of the associated difficulties. Wynne Harlen reminds us about this when she says:

Observation is the process through which we come to take notice, to become conscious, of things and happenings. It can involve the use of any of the senses, alone or in combination. But taking in information by observation is not like soaking up water into a sponge. The senses do not absorb everything that is there; they function selectively, and the selection is influenced by existing ideas and expectations. Our existing concepts and knowledge affect what we see or hear or feel. For instance, two people observing the same formation of clouds in the sky may observe quite different things about them. One, who knows little about clouds except that they block out the sun and bring rain, may see only their extent across the sky and their darkness. Another, who knows the significance of different features of clouds, may be able to report on their probable height, depth, direction of movement, changing formation and be able to predict further changes from these observations. (Harlen, 1985)

She goes on to describe the well-known story of the local vicar and the entomologist who are walking in the churchyard on a pleasant summer's evening. The choir are fervently practising in the vestry and their singing mingles with the noise of the crickets and other early evening countryside noises. The vicar comments most positively about the delightful sound they were hearing. The entomologist agreed, and said, 'and it's wonderful to think that it comes from their back legs'. Though the physical sounds were available to both, what each heard was different.

In the process of observation and making judgement and assessment about children's activities it is important that if we see different things we are able to explain and justify our interpretations. As Joan Dean suggested in 1983, one way of improving our observations is to look at children and their work with other teachers who, because they are different people, will see and observe things differently and thus enlarge and extend our seeing.

The More You Look The More You See

I hope by now you are convinced that improved observation is one way of improving assessment, but that this is more than a knee-jerk response to current demands and accountability. As Stephen Rowland has suggested, there is a great deal to be gained in terms of understanding the individual children in our charge.

> From my experience of working on my own in a classroom, I had begun to realize that whenever I looked really closely at what the children were doing, the choices they were making and the forms of expression they were using, then a picture began to build up of a child who was, in some sense, more 'rational' than I had previously recognized. It seemed that, the closer I looked, not only the more I saw, but the more intelligent was what I saw. (Rowland, 1984)

In a later article, which considers classroom enquiry as a way of understanding children's learning, he goes on to consider the implications, given the typical classroom situation with thirty or more children often involved in a wide variety of activities, and only one teacher. In such a context, he suggests, much of our interpretation has to be undertaken rapidly, often on the spur of the moment. The speed with which decisions are often made allows little time for reflection:

For this reason, the interpretations we make in the classroom are likely to be based upon rules of thumb and everyday assumptions about the children and the subject matter which we use uncritically. A more careful investigation of what children's activity really means requires not only time but a certain 'intellectual space': an opportunity to reflect, preferably with others, and to develop and share insights into the children's concerns, skills and understandings. Certainly, we cannot reflect with this degree of intensity upon all the children's work, nor even upon a major proportion of it. Nevertheless, the in-depth study of selected samples of activity from our classrooms can lead us to challenge, modify and at times radically alter those assumptions from which we work when we interact with children in the classroom. It can help us build an understanding of the learning process and of the concerns of children which are expressed and developed through that process. We must develop such understanding if we are to realize our role as educators rather than merely as purveyors of knowledge. (Rowland, 1986)

It is the attempt to study in depth and analyze such selected examples of children's activities and classroom products that will help us in the process of assessment. A recent article by Gipps and Goldstein has argued for the development of a curriculum for teacher assessment. They argue:

Assessment is a tool for teachers, to be used for the benefit of students. It should be developed so that the obverse of competition and global comparisons is one of feedback, enhanced awareness and motivation. This is sound pedagogical practice, and is also one way of enhancing (some may say restoring) the professional role of teachers. (Gipps and Goldstein, 1989: 504)

A recent in-service course that colleagues and I have been involved in has taken the need for realism in classroom assessment as a serious requirement. In the introductory material describing the course it was recognized that teachers have always been aware of the need to monitor their children's learning, and one of the most far-reaching effects of the Education Reform Act will be to make the process of assessment — in all its forms — a central feature of school accountability. The introduction of new programmes of study and their associated attainment targets will necessarily involve teachers in new forms of assessment, but it was regarded as important to recognize and value the knowledge and skills teachers already possess. So the course drew upon teachers' experiences in their own schools and classrooms, using their first-hand observations and written records as the material upon which the course was based. It was used to investigate the dilemmas and tensions experienced by teachers, for example: between the expressed expectations of society in the National Curriculum and the needs of individual children; between testing attainment targets and the growth of the whole child; between measuring achievement and monitoring the quality of everyday classroom experiences; between providing information to parents as 'clients' and as 'partners'.

Throughout the course, there was an emphasis upon cooperative and collaborative learning. Members of the group were encouraged to learn from the expertise of their colleagues on the course and to take responsibility for contributing to the process of learning in the whole group.

The course took the development of the skills of observation of and reflection upon classroom situations as the major arena for investigation, and addressed some of the following:

> the observation of individuals/small groups/whole classes;
> the analysis of observations;
> the process of moderation;
> the relation between informal observations and attainment targets;
> the process of recording and reporting assessments;
> self-evaluation and pupil profiling;
> communication with parents.

What follows is reflection upon that experience by one of the course members as she attempted to put the ideas she learned into practice in her own classroom and to extend what she had learned beyond her classroom to her colleagues in school and others in her locality. She also draws this chapter together with some suggestions to support teachers in the process of learning to use assessment for the benefit of both teachers and learners.

Assessment Through Classroom Observation*
(Doreen Ponting, Deputy Head Teacher, Gothic Mede Lower School, Bedfordshire)

Assessment and all its implications have caused more stress to the classroom teacher than any of the Government's reforms. The responsibility of 'labelling' a youngster at 7, 11, 14 and the increasing likelihood of baseline assessment at the incredible age of 5, is a daunting prospect for any caring professional. The teachers of today have lived through and are scarred by the exam-orientated curriculum. Little wonder, then, that when one attends

---

*This extract also appears in an article in *The Curriculum Journal*, Vol. 1, No. 2, 1990.

INSET courses for assessment, it is to find the leader faced with a wall of icy aggression from teachers. Understandably, perhaps, when one realizes that these courses are often twilight sessions after an arduous day in the classroom, the hard-pressed teacher turns on the leader who is advocating assessment through observation as a possible way forward. The children he/she has left are eager for the *next* step. Where do you find the time to stand back and watch? How can it be done alongside the multitudinous challenges of a busy classroom? Teachers become more and more despondent as demands are increased and the way to meet them is not clear.

I was fortunate enough to spend a term at the Cambridge Institute, released for one day a week to study 'Observation and its possible effects on the assessment process'. I can only try to explain the learning path I travelled and some of the valuable things I learned as a possible way through the maze. I learned:

1. To value my own experience and judgement about my children, based on evidence about them I collected through close observation.
2. The value of knowing what a child *can* do at any given moment in time measured against his own abilities, and *not* those of others.
3. The value of organizing myself to document incidental occurrences of importance in the classroom, as well as actually organizing specific assessment tasks which were embedded in ongoing learning.
4. The absolute necessity of being able to think positively about the whole business of assessment and making it a meaningful part of curriculum planning.

As a result of participating in the course, my brief was 'To devise a cross-curriculum form of assessment' for the school as a whole. This was a different proposition! For a long while it seemed almost an impossible task. As staff we had become over-burdened by records — many of which were very valuable, but not at all economic of teacher-time. We were halfway towards keeping a sort of 'profile', limited though it was, for each child. However, access to information meant wading through twelve record sheets and samples of children's work. As I sorted through the puzzle it became evident that separation of evidence and records was necessary. Factual evidence could be kept in a profile form, but the information gathered could be produced in a clear, factual, see-at-a-glance record which detailed all that could be learned about the child from this evidence.

We decided on an initial 'profile' sheet to be drawn up after the first few weeks in school. The evidence for this sheet was to be gathered from Nursery records, parental interviews, observations of the children at work, and discussion with the children themselves. Next we decided on a termly formative sheet, and, lastly, a yearly sheet which was an amalgam of all that had been learned about that child during the year. The evidence was to be kept in a folder inside an expanding wallet for ease of access during busy moments.

The implications for us now are:

1. The creation of time for assessment, and seeing it as a shared responsibility.
2. (a) Creative use of time: e.g. doubling-up, team-teaching, etc.
   (b) Extra staffing: there is no way one teacher can keep up the evidence needed unless s/he has help and non-contact time to decipher the material.
   (c) More use of other adults in the classroom itself, which is carefully planned and coordinated.
3. Detailed planning, both short-term and long-term, and the use of intermittent assessments, building into a whole profile.
4. The involvement of parent and child in the gathering of relevant information throughout the school life of the child.
5. The acceptance that observation of our children will also involve observations of our own teaching skills and classroom management. We must use this positively to improve the learning in which we are all involved.
6. INSET based on the importance of:
   (a) collaborative learning
   (b) efficient management of resources
   (c) children as independent learners
   (d) open-ended and investigative tasks, which in my limited experience afford the best results for assessment through observation
   (e) the training of staff in the skills of observation, and the realization that *factual* evidence is necessary, not judgemental or subjective comments
   (f) the training of staff to help us to interpret the various levels in children's development in specialist areas, and so to be able to use informed judgements when moderation becomes part of the procedure.

During the next few arduous years we must lean on and support each other. If we win in the assessment arena we will indeed have earned the right to be called 'Professionals', but we cannot do it alone. The funding of INSET is vital. I was able to attend the course through funding by the school pyramid and have been given the opportunity to report back to the heads and some staff of those schools. In the light of liaison between schools this must be a positive move.

The dangers of LMS loom ahead of us, with all its shortcomings and lack of resources. Far-sighted heads will see the value of stretching their purses to cater for longer-term courses such as the one I attended.

Observation is only one source of evidence. The next section goes on to consider alternative ways of gaining access to children's understanding and provide more detailed evidence upon which our judgements might be more justifiably based.

Chapter 5

Other Ways In: A Research-based Approach to Assessment

> Effective curriculum development of the highest quality depends
> on the capacity of teachers to take a research stance to their own
> teaching . . . a dispostion to examine one's own practice critically
> and systematically. (Ruddock and Hopkins, 1983: 156)

The principle advocated for curriculum development in the comment above
is also of considerable significance as far as assessment is concerned. By
adopting a 'research stance' for our teaching we can begin to develop the
skills necessary for effective as well as more reliable and valid judgements of
children's achievements. It is important that we engage in this process, for as
Jane Abercrombie reminded us in Chapter 4, it is very easy to assume
incorrectly that what you judge to have taken place actually took place;
similarly, John Elliot's suggestion in Chapter 4 that looking at a situation, an
activity, or a response from as many perspectives as possible is likely to
increase the probability of its more fairly reflecting what has occurred. The
demands that our judgements are based upon evidence applies not only to
the assessment context. Walker reminds us that reflection and enquiry are
now seen as essential elements of the teachers' role:

> As teaching has become increasingly professionalized and the
> management of educational organizations more systematized, so
> 'inquiry' has increasingly become something that teachers are
> expected to include in their repertoire of skills. (Walker; 1985)

This does not necessarily mean detailed knowledge of the literature of a
specific area or high levels of proficiency in the skills conventionally required
by testing and survey research, but is more concerned with what is needed to

cope with immediate issues in one's own institution: how to gather evidence upon which to achieve an *informed* rather than an *intuitive* judgement. Langeveld reminds us that essentially this is a practical activity:

> Educational studies are 'a practical science' in the sense that we do not only want to know facts and to understand relations for the sake of knowledge. We want to know and understand in order to be able to act and act 'better' than we did before. (Langeveld, 1965)

This can be applied at a variety of levels and in a variety of contexts. For example, it can include:

> an attempt to evaluate what is presently occurring in a particular activity or situation;
> an attempt to find out what is actually happening, recognizing, as Abercrombie (1969) point out, that what actually occurs need not necessarily be what is thought to be occurring;
> an attempt to support, extend or influence the progress and processes of something newly introduced into the school or curriculum.

Lewis and Munn have suggested that

> The overall aim of these kinds of investigations is usually to provide some systematic and reliable information that can be used as a basis for action. Instead of relying upon intuition and value-judgements in making decisions, the individual teacher, the department or the school staff as a whole can use carefully collected evidence to feed into the decision-making process. (Lewis and Mann, 1987)

There are clearly varying levels at which this might be applied. For example, Walker has identified the following range of concerns:

> An individual teacher may have identified a problem, an interest, or a concern within his or her own classroom and wish to find out more to resolve a dilemma. This may be related to an individual child, group of children, an aspect of assessment or classroom management.
> A group of teachers may wish to review a range of alternative curriculum proposals to judge their likely impact in practice.
> A school staff may need to evaluate practice, performance and policy in teaching and in administration.
> There may be a need to provide evidence and analysis of the school's programme for management purposes or to inform the LEA, school governors, parents and others.

There is also likely to be a need to interpret and to assess information coming into schools from a variety of sources — central government, the examination boards, the LEA, HMI, NCC, SEAC or the academic world.

Also, there is a need to make effective use of information provided by agencies that are concerned with pupils but do not necessarily share educational assumptions or use the language of schooling: eg., the social services, the MSC, employers. (Walker, 1985)

Investigations of these kinds are all aimed at improving the context for children's learning — a concern shared by the assessment process. As an important principle, the aim should be that such enquiries are undertaken collaboratively as a means of supporting each other and learning from each other. There is mounting evidence to show that shool improvement can occur when teachers are active partners in determining priorities for development and policies for their implementation. Ainscow and Conner have suggested elsewhere that:

In the current situation the need for teachers to have effective strategies for developing aspects of their practice is particularly important. Recent legislation, particularly the 1988 Education Act, has led to a range of new initiatives that require teachers to learn new skills and work within new constraints. Processes of collaborative inquiry and development can be a powerful way of helping individual teachers to respond to these requirements. (Ainscow and Conner, 1990:1)

In addition to observation, there are a number of other 'effective strategies' that have been adopted for classroom investigations which are likely to prove useful in the development of assessment skills amongst teachers.

The diagram below from Hook provides an overview of those typically associated with investigation in classrooms. The following have proved particularly useful for the development of assessment strategies and collecting information to support judgements:

narrative Records
audiotaping and transcription
videotaping and analysis of activities
discussions and interviews with children
self-assessment.

Figure 5.1: Hook's Summary of Approaches to Studying Classrooms

Method	Personnel and equipment	Advantages	Disadvantages	Examples of use
Observation instruments	By teacher, colleague or outsider Note book, recording sheets, checklists, etc.	Fits in with regular school activities Selective focus Economical as regards money and equipment First-hand information about actual behaviours Adaptable to individual classroom situations Can be used in live situations or with audio or video records	Can interfere with teaching and classroom management Difficult to be fully objective May need support equipment for complete analysis, e.g. tape recorder Colleagues or outsiders may not be available to help May need to be carried out over an extended period	Analysis of teacher questioning, pupil response, pupil-pupil interaction Pupil participation in activities Use of equipment by pupils Estimation of pupil achievement and performance levels Teacher and pupil movement Playground behaviour
Field notes, anecdotal records and diaries	By teacher Note book, record cards or sheets, diary	Personal viewpoints Can be compiled by the participant observer at any time Uncomplicated and cheap Can be incorporated into self-analysis of day's work and future lesson planning. Cumulative records enable analysis for patterns, trends, etc. Other evidence can easily be added to notes or records	Subjective impressions and accounts may be biased More objective analysis may need other data collection techniques Detailed or long conversations are difficult to record by hand	Implementation of new curriculum package Account of pupil's behaviour at school camp Self-reflection about own teaching techniques Introduction of team teaching and effect on teachers and pupils Workings of school council

Figure 5.1: continued

Interview	By teacher or outsider with teacher, pupils, parents, etc. Note book, tape recorder	Face-to-face contact with informant Comfortable, informal approach Can use during school or after school Suitable for in-depth probing and/or identification of problems or needs Direct approach — can be adjusted to respondent's age or language level	Time-consuming Some pupils may have difficulty expressing their views, or may be reluctant to reveal true feelings Ousider may be unfamiliar with pupils or parents	Obtaining pupils', other teachers' or parents' views about classroom and school matters, e.g. reading scheme, new equipment, school rules, teaching methods, etc.
Questionnaire	By teacher with pupils, other teachers, parents and community Question sheet	Easily distributed Can be quick to fill in Focused and adaptable to specific needs Provides feedback for action Respondents familiar with questionnaire procedures	Preparation can be lengthy Clear and relevant answers require careful preparation and trial runs Analysis of responses is time-consuming May get poor rate of return Difficult to get in-depth responses — may need to be supplemented by interview Problems of obtaining true or honest responses from pupils	Expectations of pupils about a new curriculum or subject Pupils' comments about instruction or school organization Parents' views about school policy, curriculum content, etc. Teachers' opinions about school equipment, organization, etc.

Figure 5.1: continued

Sociometric methods	By teachers with pupils Question sheet	Reveal pupils' interpersonal relationships Adaptable to specific circumstances and needs Ease of construction and administration	Pupils may be reluctant to reveal true feelings unless confidentiality is assured Do not give reasons for pupils' choices Short-term — need to be repeated periodically Unsuitable for groups who do not know each other	Groupings of pupils for cooperative work Seating in classroom Deciding partners for classroom activities
Unobtrusive measures	By teacher Note book, camera	Inexpensive, straightforward approach Can supplement other methods through triangulation Do not affect school or classroom environment- non-reactive Draw on a variety of evidence	Some evidence may be inaccessible, e.g. confidential documents Need to develop skill in being unobtrusive! May be accused of invasion of privacy	Pupils' attitude to school Quality of school-community relations School organization and administration
Photographs and slides	By teacher or outsider Camera (possibly plus synchroniser, slide projector and tape recorder)	Fresh perspectives on familiar settings Enable illustration of school and classroom activities Promote understanding and stimulate discussion Can be viewed by a variety of audiences	Cost of equipment Possible disruption of classroom teaching Difficult to show whole classes Selective focus of photographer Processing time — delayed feedback Purely visual, no sound (can be overcome with tape-slide methods)	Record of teacher and pupil behaviour, e.g. non-verbal expressions, cooperative work Classroom activities and out-of-school excursions and visits

Figure 5.1: continued

Audio-recording	By teacher or outsider Tape recorder, microphones	Easy to set up Records all conversation within range of equipment Portable — can be placed in different parts of room Relatively unobtrusive Allows repeated analysis	Recording is unselective — extraneous noise may mask conversation High cost of quality equipment Transcription costly and time-consuming No visual record — periods of silence convey little information	Analysis of teacher and pupil talk Recording of interviews Analysis of team teaching conferences — instructional planning Record of pupils' work
Video-recording	By teachers, pupils or outsider Camera, video-recorder, TV monitor, operator	Extensive coverage of classroom activities — sound and vision Attractive to viewers Video recordings can be viewed repeatedly, allowing a variety of analyses	Very expensive May be difficult to borrow or hire equipment Difficult to make unobtrusive	Analysis of teacher and pupil behaviour, e.g. teacher instruction, pupil group discussion, classroom movement Out-of-classroom activities, e.g. playground behaviour
Case study	By teacher or outsider Equipment and techniques previously described	Permits focus on an individual case, e.g. pupil, teacher, classroom, school, curriculum scheme In-depth analysis possible Draws on a wide variety of research methods Suitable for longitudinal or developmental approaches	Investigation in depth requires much planning, collection of information and analysis Very time-consuming if extensive coverage required Feedback to teacher may be delayed until case study completed	Study of single case, e.g. pupil, new instructional approach, maths curriculum package, school assessment procedures, etc

(Hook, 1985)

Narrative Records

The National Curriculum is going to require that teachers keep careful records of children's progress on each attainment target for the purposes of reporting to parents. A narrative form of recording particularly suitable for teachers to use to gather evidence upon which later judgements might be based is what Hook described in 1985 as the 'anecdotal record', a kind of diary or regular series of notes on exactly what a child or children did or said in a given situation. Such a record can provide an objective and longitudinal picture of the change or lack of change in children's achievements. Wrightstone describes the process in the following way:

> As successive objective observations accumulate, the record contains a variety and continuity of evidence which may yield a tentative picture of the child's behaviour patterns and growth, his interests and attitudes, his strengths or weaknesses and his problems . . . Anecdotal records are reports of current observations of specific incidents which illustrate the child's reactions . . . and give a cumulative picture of the child's growth. (Wrightstone, 1960: 931)

A growing number of teachers is attempting to gather evidence in this way, using individual record cards or a record book with several pages for each child. As something pertinent occurs it is noted down for reflection later on. David Hopkins (1985) suggests that keeping a record in this way is not very time-consuming and provides surprisingly frank information that is built up over time.

Some teachers are happy for this to happen incidentally, whilst others prefer to adopt a more systematic approach, focusing upon specific children for a period of time, perhaps during a week, followed by another group the following week. If particularly important issues arise for children not in focus during this time, that is, of course, noted.

Zimmerman and Wieder (1977) suggest a *what? when? where? how?* formula for structuring diary records. The *what?* involves a description of the activity; *when?* involves reference to the time and timing of the activity, with special attention to recording the *actual* sequence of events; *where?* involves a designation of the location of the activity, suitably coded so that it can be noted quickly; the *how?* involves a description of whatever logistics were entailed by the activity.

Brandt (1972) advocates the following procedure:

> Record any pertinent incident as soon as possible after the event to ensure accuracy and comprehensiveness;

include the date, time, setting, who was involved, and a description of
what happened;

use direct comments wherever possible;

the entry should attempt to be a factual record, not a judgement of the
event.

A number of advantages and disadvantages of anecdotal records have been
identified (Bieker, 1950; Hook, 1985; Hopkins, 1985; Bell, 1987).

1. The child is monitored in his/her own terms and the procedure
   offers a way of improving our understanding of each child.
2. Evidence can be gathered about a wide variety of behaviour.
3. The records are very simple to keep and require no outside help.
4. They provide a useful, on-going, continuous record.
5. They may be used by individual teachers, groups, or the whole
   school as an in-service training device.
6. They offer an opportunity to learn through participation.
7. They require no special training and may be suited to the approach
   of each individual teacher.
8. The teacher can increase accuracy and recognize her own bias by
   checking against the viewpoints of others.
9. The teacher learns to convert impressions and judgements into
   accurate data, which can be used as a growing body of evidence to
   understand why a child behaves as s/he does, and report
   assessments fairly and reliably.
10. The teacher may learn to reserve judgement and attain greater
    objectivity about situations which are difficult to interpret.
11. The experience encourages the teachers to gain respect for the
    children's ability and for their own skills of thinking, reflection and
    observation.
12. Experience with anecdotal records may encourage a teacher to have
    closer relations with children, both personally and professionally.

In fact, experience of working with teachers who have attempted to keep
such records suggests that their observations and the information gathered
begin quickly to influence the content and organization of future learning
experiences. Jo-Anne Reid describes her experience of keeping such a record:

Last year I started to keep a journal — not a pretty one with dates
and space limitations on the pages, but a purple government-issue
exercise book. And I only started keeping it because somebody
told me to: it was one of the requirements of the Language and
Learning course I was involved in. It was to help with reflection
upon what we were learning, and as I soon found out, the

reflection became one of the most important parts of the learning process itself. It was in my journal that I was able, at my own speed and in my own words, to come to terms with what I had found out, and so make clear to myself what I did know, had learnt, or was still unsure about. Writing in the journal also made me feel good — I had so much to say, so many new and old ideas juggling in my mind, just waiting for me to sort them, make links between them, and so organize them. The act of thinking and writing them down seemed to make this easy — and at the same time the pleasure that came from seeing how much I had to say about the ideas made it extremely rewarding. (Reid, 1984: 173)

All the problems of the classroom; all the ideas I had, or the students had, for improving things; organizational matters; my doubts about what I was doing; plans for the future; all these were sorted out and worked over in my journal. My thoughts about students, other teachers, the school as a whole, were written down (exorcised?) to the extent that my journal became a sounding board, and writing my journal became almost a form of therapy. I felt better after writing — I felt that I could work out what I needed to work out, and that, having made my thoughts, fears, plans, criticisms, concrete, by writing them down, I was much more able to act upon what I had decided was best. I felt my teaching was improving. (ibid.:174)

Advice on keeping diaries and anecdotal records can be found in two recent publications: *Writing to Grow* by Mary Louise Holly, published by Heinemann (1989); and *Teachers' own Records. A System Promoting Professional Quality* by Elizabeth Adams and Tyrrell Burgess, published by NFER — Nelson (1990).

Disadvantages and Common Errors

Initially, developing an appropriate means of keeping anecdotal records can be time-consuming. The important thing is to develop a procedure that suits you and uses time efficiently. Unless some structure is introduced, it is difficult to ensure that such records are collected for the whole class and an appropriate range of activities, and unless we are prepared to share our comments with others they can easily become rather subjective. Brandt identifies some common errors in this context. Anecdotal records, he suggests (1972), often include interpretations and evaluations of the incident rather than accurate description, so they can appear as little more than a series of personalized reactions. Also, they sometimes contain only positive or negative episodes, reflecting the bias of the observer. If we can develop our skills in overcoming these weaknesses, anecdotal records can provide a powerful source of evidence to support the assessments we undertake in our classrooms.

Audiotaping and Transcribing

Hook recognizes that:

> A fundamental problem facing the teacher wishing to observe his/her classroom and the effects of teaching on children's learning is that in most situations it is not possible to take the role of an observer systematically recording and describing what is happening. There are occasions when the teacher is not directly involved in activities and as a result it is possible to observe behaviour, listen to conversations and discuss with individuals in an attempt to understand the complexities of a situation. However, there are normally few opportunities for extended periods of uninterrupted observation. One solution to the problem of observing one's own classroom, teaching behaviour, or children's activities is to use technical devices to record classroom events. (Hook, 1985)

One other weakness of anecdotal recording not mentioned previously is that it is not always possible to note down exactly what an individual has said in an assessment situation. Sometimes, using audiotaping to support the collection of evidence contributes further to our understanding of children's competence. An increasing number of teachers is using tape recorders in their classrooms as part of school-based in-service activities, and children quickly become used to tape recorders being used and using them themselves. Once children are used to tape recorders these provide an opportunity for the teacher to monitor the progress of thinking of a group as well as individuals within a group over a sustained period of time. They provide information to support or question the assumption made through our often fleeting contacts with children in a busy classroom. Provided that the use of the tape recorder has been carefully prepared, i.e. that it works, that the acoustics are reasonable, and that it is possible to differentiate between the children's voices, it can successfully monitor conversations during activities without the teacher's presence. The use of a radio-microphone allows much clearer recordings to be collected and can allow both teachers and children considerably more freedom of movement around the classroom.

Once the tape recording has been made it can be used in a number of ways. Hook has argued that the use of sound enables the listener to concentrate on the nature of the conversation, on the mode of expression adopted, as well as the understanding of content or meaning that each individual demonstrates. As he suggests:

> The audiotape provides a semi-permanent record of inter-changes which can be reviewed and analysed many times over in a multiplicity of ways. (Hook, 1985)

Although sound recordings of classroom activities provide valuable information, the production of transcripts of the conversations enables more detailed analysis of the events that have taken place. As Hopkins has commented:

> Transcripts are excellent for those situations where teachers require a very specific and accurate record of a particular interaction. (Hopkins, 1985)

It must be remembered, however, that transcription is time-consuming. Judith Bell (1987) suggests that in general one should allow up to ten hours for one hour of tape recording! It is also the case that, in transcribing, valuable information such as expression, tone, and pacing of comment can easily be lost, and misinterpretation can occur. Occasionally, however, selected extracts taken from a tape recording can provide useful evidence to support our judgements. The most appropriate activity for us to engage in is to create opportunities for listening carefully to the tape recordings. They can provide endless entertainment in traffic jams if you have a cassette in your car as you drive to and from school. By careful listening, you get to know the processes of children's thinking much more effectively. This can improve our assessments as well as our planning of future learning activities.

Hitchcock and Hughes offer some useful advice for the process of transcription:

1. Listen to the complete tape at least twice through without attempting to write anything down. This will provide the transcriber with a sense of the materials as a whole, the rhythm, tone, and substantive content of the talk together with an 'ear' for who is talking at what point.
2. The use of headphones gets the researcher or transcriber closer to the data and eliminates any distracting extraneous background noise.
3. Transcribing proper will involve listening to short 'chunks' of talk and noting it down, and playing and replaying the tape backwards and forwards in order to get an accurate transcript.

4. Once a reasonable transcript has been made from the tape the researcher or transcriber should listen to the tape again as a whole while going through her own transcript of it and making any additions or corrections as she goes along, stopping the tape at the appropriate points in order to facilitate this.
5. If possible, it is always useful to get another person to listen to the tape and cross-check the transcript. (Hitchcock and Hughes, 1989:167)

One other important comment about audio recording concerns the stimulus for discussion, especially when the children have had sufficient experience to work alone or in small groups. Thea Prisk's experience with 6-year-olds (1987) demonstrates that a poem can create an amazing amount of reflective discussion. She provided a small group with a complex poem and asked the children what it was about, and whether they would mind taping their ideas. The results were beyond her expectations of the children's knowledge and understanding and caused her to rethink her views of the children's potential.

Another useful way of stimulating discussion is to use photographs of classroom events, and invite the children to comment on what was happening, what they were doing and what they thought others in the photograph were doing. Such an activity not only reveals knowledge and understanding, but can offer useful evaluation about the appropriateness of learning activities.

Hook, although a keen advocate of the tape recorder in classrooms, emphasizes that there are important disadvantages. A single tape recorder in the middle of a group of children might capture all that has been said, but even if you know the children it is still often difficult to separate comments out and attribute them correctly to individuals.

Obtaining a clear, audible sound recording is probably the most difficult and elusive thing to achieve in monitoring classroom activities. The human ear is so much more sensitive, selective and discriminating than most microphones. (Hook, 1985)

Given this comment, it is often a useful complementary activity to use the tape recorder as a back-up to our observations. It provides us with a means of checking what a child actually said, rather than what we think he or she said. We can also listen to the tape recordings from a position of some knowledge of the events that have taken place.

Ireland and Russell offer a series of wise words on recording:

It's best to use a cassette tape recorder with an automatic level control. Locate the recorder closer to students than to the teacher...the teacher's voice is always the loudest. Try the recorder when the classroom is empty to make sure it is working; it's very disappointing to make the effort of recording, only to find that the tape is blank or inaudible. (Ireland and Russell, 1978:21)

Video-recording

An increasing number of primary schools either own or have access to a video-camera. The facility that video-recordings of children's activities offers to improving our assessments is endless. Audio-recordings lose information as to non-verbal cues, children's facial expressions, their body movements, and the behaviour of other speakers and non-speakers. Video-recording suffers from none of these disadvantages, and can provide a comprehensive means of monitoring children's activities. Synchronized sound and vision and the possibility of playing either sound or vision independently offer excellent resources for teachers engaged in assessment of children's learning. They also provide means by which an individual teacher's judgement can be compared with the views of other colleagues via a group viewing session and follow-up discussion. As with audio-recording, it is not possible or potentially useful for this to happen all the time. Occasional inclusion of video-recording as part of a programme of assessments adds to the 'triangulation' of our interpretations. Triangulation, it will be remembered, was a procedure advocated by John Elliott (Chapter 4), and has been described in the following way;

A particularly useful strategy for checking information is known as *triangulation*. Put simply, this means the use of two or more sets of information to study the one event or process. It may, for example, involve comparing and contrasting information using different methods (e.g., observation and video-recording, or by taking account of the views of different people). (Ainscow and Conner, 1990).

The potential of the video-camera in this context is recognized by Jardine when he suggests:

With videotape, we can make recordings of inter-personal communications, replay them, and invite each person involved to talk us through what he sees himself doing and what he sees others doing. His new perspective on his own and the others' actions is based upon a complete behavioural record which is common reference for each person. Each person's experience will still, of necessity, be selective, but the selection is open to checking and modification in the light of subsequent replays and of the perspectives of others. (Jardine, 1972:27)

Adams and Biddle (1970) claim three major advantages for the use of videotape. Firstly, it provides a comprehensive record of an activity or of classroom events that can be preserved for subsequent analysis. Then, the 'fidelity' of the system is extremely positive, which means that the camera can deal with a variety of situations and that the microphones are able to pick up a great many of the public utterances that take place. Thirdly, the stop-rewind facility permits sequences of behaviour to be reviewed at will.

If an observer or colleague can be persuaded to operate the recorder, then more attention can be paid to the totality of any assessment situation. i.e., not only the part played by the children, but also the effects of the teacher. It is important to recognize, however, that the video records only that which it is aimed at; thus, the operator acts as an editor of what is excluded as well as what is included (Walker, 1985).

If the video becomes a regular feature of the children's classroom experience, it also enables the teacher to build up a comprehensive picture over time of the progress within his/her classroom. The systems now available represent the most sophisticated facilities available to those wishing to focus on their own classrooms or teaching; they are relatively easy to operate; and can be powered from either a battery or mains supply. Although the purchase price is high, video-equipment is comparatively inexpensive to run, and tapes can be reused many times. With the use of a wide-angled lens, a camera can view complete classes or focus on individual pupils. As a result, video-recordings offer the opportunity to capture a great deal of what is going on in the classroom and offer teachers the opportunity to '...increase personal awareness through self-confrontation and self-analysis' (Hook, 1985). Hook goes on to suggest:

1. Teachers can see and hear what they are doing from a fresh perspective.
2. Teachers can examine carefully the behaviour of pupils, particularly in relation to teacher-actions.
3. Teachers can look for discrepancies between observed and desired performance.

Video-cameras can operate under quite poor light conditions, but sound recording is never simple in the classroom setting. The use of a radio microphone can ensure the adequate recording of pupil responses.

McGrew made extensive use of video-recordings with children and suggested the following as useful precursors to using video:

have the equipment assembled before the children arrive;
allow them to inspect it freely;
think carefully about the positioning of the camera;
move around slowly when recording. (McGrew, 1976)

Hopkins notes two major weaknesses in the use of video-cameras in the classroom. The first, of course, is cost, but this is getting easier with the current 'Cam Corders', as well as provision for borrowing from local teachers' centres. The other is that the 'intrusiveness, even invasiveness of some equipment can have a disruptive effect on the classroom'. If McGrew's comments, offered earlier, are subscribed to, Hopkins believes that:

> ... the novelty-value of the equipment rapidly disappears with use. I advise teachers to introduce the equipment to pupils first, demonstrate how it works, and then leave it standing in the classroom sometime before actually taping. This allows both pupils and teachers to become accustomed to its presence. (Hokpins, 1985:70)

To avoid interfering with the children's activities when recording, McGrew (1972) suggested that teachers should maintain distance, not get involved, avoid facing the child or children being studied. 'Never fix your gaze on the child, because it can raise his/her awareness that they are the focus of attention.' The major justification of using video-recording in the classroom comes from Hook when he comments:

> Perceptive self-reflection supported by reasoned judgement is frequently evident in those practised in viewing their own behaviour. From initial problems with 'cosmetic effects', anxiety and often unwarranted self-criticism, comments of teachers develop into objective, constructive analyses of teaching strategies and pupil-behaviour. (Hook, 1985:248)

Discussions/Interviews with Children

There is an increasing tendency to involve children in the process of assessment. The *Inner London Education Authority Primary Language Record* (ILEA, 1989) includes a discussion with each child as a central feature of the monitoring of their linguistic competencies. Also, the recent evaluation of the *Profiling and Records of Achievement Pilot Schemes* (PRAISE, 1989) endorses the benefits to be gained from engaging children in discussion about their progress, suggesting that they were able to contribute valuable information towards their assessment. Hook believes that the value of discussion and interviews lies in the opportunity provided for gathering information about knowledge, feelings and attitudes, expectations and intentions and actions and reasons for these actions. He describes interviewing as an art, a skilled technique developed over time and through practice. With increasing confidence it becomes an adaptable means of gaining access to children's perceptions.

> Successful interviewers are those with flexibility, sensitivity, insight and intuition to be able to secure the maximum amount of information . . . but at the same time make the (child) feel that the information he is giving is important and beneficial. (Hook, 1985:136)

Interviews range across a continuum from the highly structured to the unstructured, or combine the qualities of these extremes by starting with a series of clearly defined questions and then on the basis of responses decide to probe and explore reasons for earlier answers.

Five main kinds of interview have been described (Hook, 1985: Cohen and Manion, 1985: Bell, 1987):

1. the structured or standardized interview, in which a predetermined set of questions is asked in a prescribed order;
2. the unstructured or unstandardized interview, an approach usually associated with counselling, guidance and clinical psychology;
3. the non-directive interview, in which the course of questioning and the topics of conversation are largely governed by the interviewee;
4. the focused interview, where attention is directed at a particular topic or theme. The focused interview is regarded as the most appropriate way of examining children's views and feelings;
5. the conversational interview. In the relaxed environment of the classroom or the playground, children can often offer telling insights which would have proved difficult or even impossible to obtain by other means.

The success or failure of an interview depends heavily on thorough preparation and an understanding of the topic to be discussed. Newson and Newson suggest:

> Although it will be clear that she has some sort of guide to work to, the good interviewer will ask the individual questions as if she had made them up at that moment because she really wanted to know the answers. The order of questions is worked out precisely, so that the conversation will have both flow and a variety of pace; and this together with a sensitive use of pausing and hesitation, facial

expression and tone of voice, allows the interviewer to maintain at least an appearance of spontaneity, naturalness and ease. (Newson and Newson, 1976: 34)

Successful interviews and interviewers have been described (Hook, 1985) as being purposeful, supportive, humorous, responsive, egalitarian, and displaying such qualities as frankness, friendliness, rapport, trust, confidentiality, spontaneity, ease, courtesy and understanding.

Walker and Adelman offer a number of useful suggestions about interviewing.

1. Try to be a sympathetic, interested and attentive listener without taking an active role. In this way you convey that you value and appreciate the child's opinion.
2. Try to be neutral. Do not express your own opinion, and be careful to avoid feelings of surprise or disapproval of the child's response.
3. If you are at ease, this will be conveyed to the children and help them to relax.
4. Reassurance is of great importance; the children need to feel sure that they are not being subject to a test and that their role is not to search out the answer in your head.
4. Great care is needed with the phrasing of questions. Donaldson (1979) reminds us that even the youngest children are able to demonstrate their competence if we discuss with them in an appropriate context, using language which they understand, and when they are clear about the purposes and intentions of the adult who is working with them. (Walker and Adelman, 1975)

The benefits of engaging children in reflective discussion about their learning was recognized by Bennett and Desforges in their study (1984) of matching learning activities to the cognitive competence of children. They attempted to help teachers to develop their learning and found that teachers tended to want to remedy weakness or mistakes that their conversation had identified, instead of accepting them as information about children's progress.

A major limitation of this process, particularly relevant to teachers, is that children may be unwilling to respond in a frank and honest fashion. They may not be prepared to reveal their true feelings or recount experiences and are unlikely to make comments that concern the teacher. Often, however, this is because of unfamiliarity with the activity; with experience the quality of dialogue can improve quite radically.

To overcome this problem, teachers need to foster an environment carefully that is supportive of children's comments and participation. Alternatively, a teacher may wish to involve another colleague who can carry out the discussion. The use of an outsider was a technique employed successfully in the Ford Teaching Project. The outsider can be another teacher, a parent, or even someone not involved in the school. Sometimes it was found that children were prepared to express themselves more openly to outsiders. The Ford Project offered the following comments about the process of interviewing children:

1. Children often need help to express themselves. The interviewer should, however, be very careful when in this situation. If too little help is given, the child may simply respond with monosyllabic answers or 'I don't know'. If too much help is given, the child may believe that you want him or her to give a specific answer. You will end up by putting the words into the child's mouth and having the child agree with what you have to say! Give help, not direction.

2. Children often respond with a 'don't know' reply in order to gain time to gather their thoughts. If you get a 'don't know' response, do not be in too much of a hurry to pass on to the next item. Wait patiently and expectantly for a short while. The child will probably then expand on his original statement.

3. The interview should be conducted very informally. Do not intimidate the child by referring constantly to clip-boards and notes. If the child believes he is being examined by you, he will only give the answers he expects you want to hear.

4. Adopt a neutral attitude throughout.

5. Make it clear to the child that you are interested only in what he or she thinks, and phrase the questions accordingly: e.g., say, 'What do you think about what happened earlier?' rather than, 'What happened earlier?'.

6. Be attentive to what the child is saying, even if the responses are being recorded. If the child gets the impression that you are not listening or are not interested in what he or she has to say, it will only impede the responses.

7. One should talk to children at their own level; this is vital. Questions must be too easy rather than too hard. Older children should be treated like young adults.

8. The child must not be laughed at or ridiculed. Wrong answers must be taken seriously and not scorned.

9. Sensitive children should preferably be interviewed on their own. Children are often very cruel and ridicule some children. This can be eliminated in part in group situations by phrasing the questions carefully, but brighter children soon realize what is happening.

10. The interview must be lively and interesting. Children soon get bored, so you mustn't 'waffle' around the point. The child must

see that you are interested in the subject, as well as him or her.

11. The interview need not always be in lesson time. Children are often very willing to give up their own time if they feel the interviewer is sufficiently interested to give up his time.

12. If the interviewer is a stranger, he must be introduced to the children and a little time given for them to relax.

13. In all interviews, a little encouragement goes a very long way.

(Adapted from K. Forsyth and J. Wood, in *Food Teaching Project, Ways of Doing Research in One's Own Classroom,* undated: 14-15)

By giving attention to such details there is great potential for learning more about each child. As Law has experienced in developing Records of Achievement:

The interview was a worthwhile experience . . . I felt I got to know the individual very well. There were plenty of surprises. Several pupils turned out to have individual skills and interests that I would never have guessed at . . .

In five minutes of interview time, I learned more about the children as individuals than in the whole of the rest of the year. (Law, 1986)

A further alternative to using an outsider is to use the children themselves to interview each other. David Hopkins (1985) suggests that pupil-interviews can provide a rich source of data. Thea Prisk's (1988) study of young children talking without the presence of teachers is testimony to the quality of information that can be obtained from even the youngest children. Allowing pupils to discuss on their own, with a tape recorder to record the content and process of their conversation, can have great advantages in that children are often more candid with each other and may produce unanticipated and often unusual information. Effectively managed, it can leave the teacher free to observe the process, which can offer further evidence to support and extend our judgements.

Of course, as with the other techniques discussed in this section, discussions of the kind described can be time-consuming, and it will not be possible to engage children in this way all of the time. It is necessary to be selective and apply the right procedure at the right time.

Self-assessment

Many primary teachers involve their children in planning work, recording activities and setting targets for learning as part of their normal classroom practice. Adding children's reflections upon and assessments of their learning seems a natural extension to these activities. There is a variety of ways in which this can be undertaken; for example, through simple questionnaires, pupil diaries and self-assessment inventories.

Hopkins suggests that questionnaires that ask specific questions about aspects of the classroom, particular curriculum experiences or the organization of learning, are an efficient way of obtaining useful information from children. With younger children it is probably more effective to use relatively simple questions with easy-to-answer procedures. He advocates the use of 'smiley' faces or cartoon features as illustrated in Figures 5.2 and 5.3. The advantage of this procedure is that they are easy and fun to complete and provide potential avenues for follow-up with the children at a later stage. Properly constructed, they can provide the teacher with information about individuals and groups on a variety of themes, and are a particularly pertinent means of gaining access to children's feelings about their progress.

Figure 5.2: '*Smiley Faces*'

(Hopkins, 1985)

Another useful way of retaining contact with the pupils' perceptions is to offer them the opportunity of keeping a regular personal diary or journal of their classroom experiences. The Writing Project (SCDC, 1988) advocated this as a way of improving relations between teachers and children as well as providing an important means of developing children's writing skills. Once the pupils feel confident about the process and are assured of confidentiality, it can become a very useful two-way process with the teacher responding to the individual comments of each child. As far as assessment is concerned, it can provide feedback from the pupils' perspective and help in the identification of individual difficulties. It involves the children in reflecting upon their experiences and can quickly become a natural part of their classroom behaviour. It is important to remember, however, that the necessary rapport takes time to get established since pupils may initially be inhibited from discussing personal issues with the teacher, and it is also a problem for younger children and those who find writing difficult to record their thoughts and feelings. As an option for some of the children, it provides another means of gaining access to their understanding.

The last few years have seen a movement in education towards methods of assessment which more directly involve the children. Such procedures

Figure 5.3: Questionnaire on Reading Progress

NAME _____ ROOM _____ TEACHER _____

1. **How do you feel when your teacher reads a story aloud?**

2. **How do you feel when someone gives you a book for a present?**

3. **How do you feel about reading books for fun at home?**

4. **How do you feel when you are asked to read aloud to your group?**

5. **How do you feel when you are asked to read aloud to your teacher?**

(After Hopkins, D., 1985: 75)

focus especially on success rather than failure, and recognize the pupil's special position in the learning equation. Richardson suggests:

> Developments such as the Oxford Certificate of Educational Achievement (OCEA) and the pupil records of achievement being promoted through vocational education rely on the consultative/tutorial role of the teacher, enabling pupils to develop views of themselves as learners and people. The primary sector is well placed to initiate this process in a systematic way because of its traditional concern with the development of the whole child. (Richardson, 1989: 41)

Richardson goes on to argue that when children are given the opportunity to review and reflect on what they have done and then discuss this with an adult, their motivation, enjoyment and understanding substantially increase.

The following extracts offer examples of the way in which individual teachers and schools have begun this process.

Figure 5.4: A Self-assessment Questionnaire

Please put a ring round the answer you wish to give to each question. If you are not sure ring the nearest to what you think.

1. How much of the lesson did you enjoy?   All of it/Some of it/None

2. How much do you think you learnt?   Nothing/Something/A lot

3. How much did you understand?   Most of it/Some of it/Nothing

4. Could you find the books, information, equipment you needed?   None/Some of it/Most of it

5. Did other people help you?   A lot/A little/Not at all

6. Did other people stop you working?   A lot/Sometimes/Not at all

7. Did the teacher help you   Enough/Not enough

8. Did the lesson last   Long enough/Too long/Not long enough

9. Was the lesson   Boring/Interesting

10. Did you need anything you could not find?   Yes/No

11. Where did you get help from?   Teacher/Group/Someone else

12. Did you find this work   Easy/Hard/Just about right

13. Write down anything which made it hard for you to learn

14. Write down anything you particularly enjoyed about this lesson

(Questionnaire designed by Roger Pols from Hopkins, D., 1985)

Figure 5.5: Conference Report

Name: _____ Grade: _____ Section: _____ Term:_____

Teacher: _____ School: _____

_____

| *WORK HABITS AND ATTITUDES* | *STUDENT* | *TEACHER* |

Do I do the best work I can?

_____

How well can I use research skills
to find information?

_____

Do I contribute meaningfully to
class discussions?

_____

Can I work independently?

_____

Do I demonstrate self-control?

_____

Do I come to class prepared?

_____

_____

Parent Comment: _____ Student signature: _____

_____ Teacher signature: _____

Figure 5.6: Self-evaluation in Mathematics

Measurement
Money 1

Name

Skill/activity	Date	Book reference	Comment
I can recognize coins I can find the value (up to £1) I can give the correct change I can play 'Supermarket Snap'	5.11.85	Book 1 pages 33–36	'When we played ''supermarket snap'' I was the shopkeeper Tasha gave me the wrong change so I had to give the rest to her'
I know how to use (and make) a ready-reckoner	8.11.85		'It was easy'
I can handle 'change'	12.11.85	Book 2 pages 41–45	'Yes it is quite easy and good.'
CHECK UP PAGE		Book 2 page 60	Score previously covered
I can deal with money situations	25.11.85	Book 3 pp. 30, 34, 44 Book 4 pp. 1–4	'It is quite easy. It was very good.' 26.11.85 Discussed idea of till receipt — asked him to produce one in the word processor
I can play the money game I can deal with large amounts of money		Book 4 p. 56	Discussed different ways of paying by making small changes to coins rather than starting again each time Has a very good grasp of using money — giving change, etc. Nov. '86
CHECK UP PAGES		Book 4 pp. 19, 31, 59	

(from Richardson, 1989)

Figure 5.7: Self-evaluation in Topic Work

Class

TOPIC RECORD SHEET — SKILLS

Name: Term:

Title: People we know   Concept: Interdependence

Skill area	Skill/activity	Comments	Teacher's evaluation
Personal development	I can take turns to speak in my group I can talk to my class	'I can do it. I have practised it. I have talked about Jesus and lots of people.'	△
Observation and classification	I can tell you who to call in different emergencies	'Yes I can. Ambulance, fire engine, police.'	△
Particular language	I know about the words: delivery, extinguish, vehicle, bill, receipt, librarian	'I delivered a letter the firemen put out the fire a car you have to pay it you get it when you pay she looks after Books.'	⟨
Communication	I can write a letter to a visitor	'Yes I can I can write a letter to a fireman.'	△
Enquiry	I can interview one of my friends	'I have interviewed a friend I have interviewed Sarah and Naomi.'	⟨
Empathy	I can describe what it feels like to be a nurse	'It feels like you're at home.'	△

Key

—	— Skill practised	Red	— Middle Infant	Brown	— 2nd Year Junior
⟨	— Some improvement	Black	— Top Infant	Orange	— 3rd Year Junior
△	— Very good progress	Green	— 1st Year Junior	Purple	— 4th Year Junior
Blue	— Reception				

(from Richardson, 1989)

Figure 5.8: Pupil Self-assessment in Language

1   What do you like most about your Language work?

2   What do you like least about your Language work?

3   Which of the following do you think you do best? (Fill in the boxes by putting a 1 against the thing you most enjoy, 2 by the second and so on).

   Writing Stories

   Discussing and Talking

   Reading on your own

   Reading in groups

   Reading to your teacher

   Puzzling out answers on worksheets

   Working from workcards

   Discovering things in the library

4   Look at the list again. Which of them would you most like to be better at — either because you are already quite good at something and want to be even better or because you find something difficult and would like to improve?

   1st choice   2nd choice

5   Here is a list of important parts of our Language work — reading aloud, reading to yourself, speaking, imaginative writing, factual writing, comprehension, solving puzzles, discussion/talking, research/project work.

   Write the two things you do best..

   Write the things you find difficult...

   (from *Preparing for Assessment* London Borough of Bromley, 1989)

Richardson comments:

> We believe that children need to learn to value their own work and achievements (as well as those of others) and to develop an awareness of what they can do. From an early age, therefore, pupils should have the opportunity to record what they think they are able to do and relate this to their actual achievements through the school's internal record system. (Richardson, 1989:35)

The next chapter goes on to consider recording, reporting and communicating assessments.

Chapter 6

Recording and Reporting Assessments

Increasingly, communication between school and parents has become a central issue in English education. The importance of good communication arises from three beliefs:

first, that parents have a right to know what goes on in the schools that their children attend;
second, that such knowledge makes for good relationships between parents and teachers; and
third, that good communication will result in improvements in learning and attitudes. (Gibson, 1986)

Of all of the features of National Curriculum assessment, the one that has created the greatest uncertainty for schools and teachers concerns the recording and reporting of assessments. The question which naturally is continually asked is, 'Is there going to be a national system of record-keeping?' The Schools Examination and Assessment Council think probably not:

At this stage, it is not expected that there will be any need to prescribe the form in which each teacher should keep records of individual pupils. (*SEAC Recorder*, 2, Summer 1989)

Similarly, paragraph 22 of the draft regulations on reporting National Curriculum attainments, published in January 1990, suggested:

The Secretary of State has no present intention to require use of a standard form of report. There are however advantages, for parents especially, in the adoption of a common format for reporting at least the core requirements . . . [An example is then offered, a copy of which is seen over page] . . . schools are encouraged to explore the use of such a framework as one element,

Figure 6.1: Report on pupil achievement

Pupil................................School...............................LEA (where applicable)...............................

Signature of Headteacher...Date..

NATIONAL CURRICULUM

1. ACHIEVEMENTS IN SUBJECTS STATUTORILY ASSESSED (END OF KEY STAGE . . .) *

	Achievement in Profile Component	Achievement in Subject Overall
English	Speaking and listening	
	Reading	
	Writing	
Mathematics	Number, algebra and measures	
	Shape, space, data handling	
Science	Exploration	
	Knowledge/understanding	

2. ACHIEVEMENTS IN SUBJECTS NOT STATUTORILY ASSESSED

Technology	
History	
Geography	
Art	
Music	
Physical Education	

*The numbered levels of achievement set out here represent summaries of more detailed information which the school will let you have if given notice that you want it. Where a pupil has been exempted from any of the relevant requirements, details are set out on an accompanying sheet.

if they so choose, of a fuller report package. The Secretary of State will review the case for a mandatory form of report in due course. (DES, 1990)

It is certainly the case that there is considerable variation in the reporting procedures adopted by primary schools in Great Britain. The Schools Council Project, *Record Keeping in the Primary School* (Clift, *et al.*, 1981) identified the following range of record-keeping activities in their survey:

day-to-day records of teacher;

forecast books;

summary records for transfer of information within the school;

transition records for the transfer of information from school to school at the end of each educational stage;

transfer records for when a pupil changes schools for reasons other than transition;

diagnostic records;

records and reports to and from the supporting welfare agencies;

reports to parents.

The conclusions of the project emphasized that '*no single record was going to suit all schools*'. The best examples were to be found in schools where the recording system actually reflected the practices in the school. As Marten Shipman commented:

> . . . records that were thorough and used with enthusiasm in the research were those that served the way teaching was organized in the school. The successful records were the last stage in the process of teaching, not the first. The dog was wagging the tail. (Shipman, 1983)

Thus, the most effective recording and reporting systems tended to emerge from the organization and structure of the teaching. The successful systems were recently designed because as teaching practices changed, so the records needed to change. They were also the result of collaboration between all the teachers in these schools, where the procedures were kept under constant review. The research also identified a number of important issues as a basis for the construction of a successful recording system. They should not demand excessive teacher time, but as far as possible should be a natural part of the teaching process. They should not be too 'jargonistic' or lengthy, nor a substitute for teacher-gossip. They should not be a device for checking up on the teacher nor used as a bureaucratic device to increase school control over the lives of children. Instead, the report had to serve a number of distinct but varied purposes. Typical reasons given by teachers involved in the Schools Council Project for keeping records were:

1. to chart pupil progress and achievement;
2. to communicate information to other teachers;
3. to ensure continuity of education throughout the school;
4. to ensure continuity on transfer to other schools;
5. to guide a replacement or supply teacher;
6. for diagnostic purposes;

7. to provide information on the success or failure of teaching methods or materials;
8. to inform interested parties — parents, psychologists, etc.;
9. to provide a general picture of the school for Heads, etc.

Some of the less-expected replies to the question concerning purpose of school records included:

10. to be used as a defence against accusations of falling standards;
11. as an insurance policy against possible hostile attacks;
12. for the Head to gain control over the classroom curriculum;
13. to keep balance in areas of study;
14. to reassure teachers that progress has been made;
15. to keep tabs on each pupil in large schools. (Clift, *et al.*, 1981)

The Education Reform Act (ERA) makes it clear that there have to be school records, and that pupils must be assessed against the attainment targets as they are introduced. The ERA also makes clear that the results of the assessment should be made available, particularly to parents. As was suggested in Chapter 1, the Inner London Education Authority report, *Improving Primary Schools* (ILEA, 1985), identified two main strands in parental reactions to assessment. Parents want to know that their child is working satisfactorily and is happy, but many are also interested in how their children are getting on compared with other children of a similar age. Bennett and Hewett make a similar comment:

> In our experience, parents often feel that they have not been given an accurate picture of how well their child is doing if they cannot compare their child's work with others in the class. As a result, they have no way of judging progress or their child's potential. (Bennett and Hewett, 1989)

Types of Record

Records can change from a teacher's personal notes on individual pupil's work to a formal collection of work completed, with a comment by teacher, pupil, and (sometimes) parent, on strengths and achievements. Between these are a variety of formal and semi-formal summaries kept by schools, all of which are used as part of the process for reporting to parents. The following examples are offered as illustrations of the different kinds of procedures that are in use and may serve as a starting point for discussion or comparison with those existing in your school. You may wish to consider the strengths and weaknesses of each of the examples offered. Those included provide examples of:

recording by diary/fieldnotes;
recording by attainment targets;
recording by checklist;
recording by previously agreed criteria on a rating scale;
recording by continua;
recording progress through shorthand procedures;
recording National Curriculum assessments.

Recording by Diary/Fieldnotes

The extract below illustrating recording by diary or fieldnotes comes from that wonderful book by Michael Armstrong, *Closely Observed Children*. In this extract we not only see the sensitive recording of Sarah's writing, but also get a glimpse of Armstrong's ability to turn over an idea, a response or a reaction in his mind to relive it, reflect upon it and learn from it. As a result it adds to his and our understanding of Sarah.

Tuesday, November 23rd.
Today Sarah finished the story about the rabbit, which she had begun yesterday. It was not till quite late in the afternoon that she completed it and then she came up to me and asked if she could read it to me. She had considerable difficulty reading it, stumbling over the words much as if she was reading from her reader. It was a sad story, she told me, the rabbit died.

'Once upon a time there was a rabbit, it was not very big at all. One day the rabbit decided to go for a bounce in the town. He had not got very far before he came to a big door, at the play school. It said "no animals allowed here". The rabbit was very sad. "No animals allowed, that's not fair at all." So he pushed the door open. Lots of children were running around in the playground, it was so exciting there. But, bang, a ball had hit the rabbit's head, he was dead. All the children ran to the rabbit, he was dead for sure. One of the little girls started to cry and then another and then another. It was very sad. You will be hearing more of the rabbit story another day.'

Sarah explained to me that she was going to write more rabbit stories, hence the ending. 'But the rabbit's dead now,' I said. 'Well perhaps it had a baby,' she replied, and later she added that she might write about the rabbit earlier, before it had been killed.

The end is a little flat but until that last sentence — and I am still wondering why she added it* — the story matches her last in its vigour and precision and also in its strangeness. This time it's the rabbit's sad fate that is so surprising, and even shocking, and Sarah was very conscious of its sadness, although when she told me how the poor rabbit died it seemed almost as if she was describing something which was independent of her will. (There was perhaps a trace of self-consciousness about Sarah's tone, as she spoke, and yet I am almost certain that yesterday when she began the story, Sarah had not intended that the rabbit should die. It seemed that the story had taken hold of her imagination and imposed its own conclusion on her, despite herself.) Once again the language is vivid and subtle, for example in expressing the rabbit's indignation, 'that's not fair *at all*'; or the children's sad confirmation of the rabbit's death, 'he was dead *for sure*'; or the slowly spreading ritual of sorrow, 'one of the little girls started to cry and then another and then another, it was very sad'; as well as in her now famous phrase, 'going for a bounce'. The clarity with which the scene in the playground is imagined seems to me remarkable and despite, or perhaps just because of, the conventional opening and the conventional character of the little rabbit, the story is deeply human. There are also certain signs of Sarah's own distinctive character, for example in the way she describes the rabbit's size — 'it was not very big at all'; somehow that seems very like Sarah and her manner and style.

Stephen and I talked about Sarah's writing at the end of the day, about her growing confidence and about the time she takes to write — a day over this one short page. The pauses, the leaving it and returning to it, the ebb and flow of writing, even of writing just a page — which however for Sarah represents a sizeable effort considering all the individual words whose spelling she has to figure out besides unravelling her plot and choosing her language — all this seems to be a necessary part of writing for Sarah and something which she must be given space and time to indulge. Yesterday I wrote that perhaps Sarah hadn't really done enough in the afternoon, spending so long on one and a half sentences. Now I think my judgement was premature.

The tale of a rabbit's death was Sarah's finest story of the year

---

*Later, a friend of mine, reading through my notes, suggested to me that perhaps Sarah just did not trust her reader to have grasped the full impact of the story.

and demonstrated many of the qualities inherent in the children's earliest narratives. It demonstrated, for example, the moral and metaphysical concerns that ran through their stories, concerns which are often present, of course, in stories written for children by adults, but which seemed to acquire a new resonance in the best of the children's own work. The story deals with the unfairness, but perhaps also the necessity, of prohibitions, with excitement transformed into tragedy, with death and sorrow. It demonstrated, also, the children's ability to explore and to express their view of life through the vivid account of particular moments in particular lives, dramatized in Sarah's story in such details as the closed door that is pushed open in defiance of its warning notice, the 'bang' that shatters the playground's excitement, the succession of crying that marks the children's sorrow. And finally, the story demonstrated the children's concern for form, for telling a story in carefully ordered prose, however tentative. The tension that is created and resolved in Sarah's story reflects her own selection and ordering of the narrative material, of plot, syntax and vocabulary. (Armstrong, M., 1980: 36–38)

Recording by Attainment Target

Since the publication of the statutory orders we have seen a plethora of recording procedures based upon National Curriculum Attainment Targets. The example illustrated here comes from an excellent publication produced by the three core subject associations in an attempt to help primary teachers. The purpose of this grid is to explore the potential and possibility of a theme or topic in terms of the attainment targets for science for the 5–7-year-olds in Key Stage 1.

Figure 6.2: Recording by Attainment Targets

Individual activities in a project: grid for mapping profile components (PC) and attainment targets (AT)

ACTIVITY...

	Potential	Actual

ENGLISH AGES 5–7

PC1- **Speaking and listening**
AT1: Pupils should demonstrate their understanding of the spoken word and the capacity to express themselves effectively in a variety of speaking and listening activities, matching style and response to audience and purpose.
PC2- **Reading**
AT2: The development of the ability to read, understand and respond to all types of writing, as well as the development of information-retrieval strategies for the purpose of study.
PC3- **Writing**
AT3: A growing ability to construct and convey meaning in written language matching style to audience and purpose.
AT4: Spelling
AT5: Handwriting, children's increasing control over the physical and design aspects of writing.

MATHEMATICS AGES 5–7

PC1- **Knowledge, skills, understanding and use of number, algebra and measuring**
AT1: Using and applying mathematics in practical tasks and real-life problems.
AT2: Number; understand number and number notation.
AT3: Number; understand number operations (addition, subtraction, multiplication and division) and make use of appropriate methods of calculation.
AT4: Number; estimate and approximate in number.
AT5: Number/algebra; recognise and use patterns, relationships, sequences and make generalisations.
AT6: Algebra; recognise and use functions, formulae, equations and inequalities.
AT7: Algebra; use graphical representation of algebraic functions.
AT8: Measures; estimate and measure quantities, and appreciate the approximate nature of measurement.
PC2- **Knowledge, skills, understanding and use of shape and space and handling data**
AT9: Using and applying mathematics; using shape and space and handling data in practical tasks and real-life problems.
AT10: Shape and space; recognise and use the properties of two-dimensional and three-dimensional shapes.
AT11: Shape and space; recognise location and use transformations in study of space.
AT12: Handling data; collect, record and process data.
AT13: Handling data; represent and interpret data.
AT14: Handling data; understand, estimate and calculate probabilities.

		Potential	Actual

SCIENCE   AGES 5-7

PC1-   **Exploration of science**
AT1:   Exploration of science; develop the intellectual and practical skills to explore the world of science . . . encourage the ability to (i) explore (ii) carry out (iii) interpret results and findings (iv) draw inferences (v) communicate exploratory tasks and experiments.

PC2-   **Knowledge and understanding**
AT2:   Variety of life; develop knowledge and understanding of the diversity and classification of past and present life forms, and of relationships . . . within ecosystems.

AT3:   Processes of life; develop knowledge and understanding of the organisation of living things and of the processes which characterise their survival and reproduction.

AT4:   Genetics and evolution; develop knowledge and understanding of variation and its genetic and environmental causes and basic mechanisms of inheritance, selection and evolution.

AT5:   Human influences on the Earth; develop knowledge and understanding of the ways in which human activities affect the Earth.

AT6:   Types and uses of materials; develop knowledge and understanding of the properties of materials and the way properties of materials determine their uses and form the basis of their classification.

AT9:   Earth and atmosphere; develop knowledge and understanding of the structure and main features of the Earth, the atmosphere and their changes over time.

AT10:   Forces; develop knowledge and understanding of forces, their nature, significance and effects on the movement of objects.

AT11:   Electricity and magnetism; develop knowledge and understanding of electric and electromagnetic effects in simple circuits, electrical devices and appliances.

AT12:   Information technology; develop knowledge and understanding of information transfer and microelectronics.

AT13:   Energy; develop knowledge and understanding of the nature of energy, its transfer and control.

AT14:   Sound and music; develop knowledge and understanding of the properties, transmission and absorption of sound.

AT15:   Light; develop knowledge and understanding of the properties and behaviour of light.

AT16:   Earth in space; develop knowledge and understanding of the relative positions and movements of the Earth, Moon, Sun and solar system within the universe.

(ASE, 1989)

Recording by Checklist

Checklists or ticklists have been a useful way of keeping a record of experiences offered to children. The example illustrated comes from a pre-reading guide produced by A. E. Tansley. The major difficulty with the tick, however, is what it means. Does it indicate achievement and understanding, or does it mean that the child has experienced something? Without the 'ticker' there to explain, the usefulness of such recording procedures is always questionable.

Figure 6.3: Recording by Checklist

Pre-reading guide (4pp) *

Pupil's name ....
Date of birth .... /........ /........

	Tick	Date observed

EMOTIONAL/SOCIAL DEVELOPMENT AND ATTITUDES
Does he/she play well with other children?
Does he/she share belongings with others?
Is behaviour stable (not easily upset)?
Does he/she concentrate on what he/she is doing?
Can he/she tolerate changes in routine without stress?
Is he/she interested in books and printed material?
Has he/she a desire to read?

SKILLS
Visual discrimination
Can he/she detect differences and similarities in shape, size and colour?
Matching: picture to picture
           picture + word to picture + word
           word only to picture + word
           word only to picture only
           word only to word only
           pairs
           shapes

Aural discrimination
Can he/she detect differences and similarities between given sounds?

Language development
Does he/she use good sentences in his/her normal conversation?
Does he/she know common nursery rhymes?
Is he/she interested in listening to stories?
Can he/she relate the main ideas of a story in sequence?
Can he/she talk about a given picture?
Can he/she describe in detail what is happening, or likely to happen, in the picture?
Can he/she talk about what he/she has seen or done?
Is he/she interested in reading signs and advertisements?

CONVENTIONS
When using a book does he/she:
   (a)   follow the front to back sequence of pages?
   (b)   follow the top to bottom sequence of lines?
   (c)   follow the left to right sequence of words?
   (d)   understand the difference between letters and words?
   (e)   understand the different forms of each letter, including capitals and lower case?

*Adapted from A.E. Tansley, *Reading and Remedial Reading* (Routledge, 1967, new ed. 1972)

Recording by Previously Determined Criteria on a Rating Scale

One way of overcoming the weaknesses of checklists is to expand the range of options for the tick.

Alan Blyth (1990) advocates the inclusion of some consideration of the way in which children's competence will be differentiated. He advocates the use of the acronym, NOFAN, a five-point scale for distinguishing between children's reactions and responses:

Never
Occasionally
Frequently
Always
Naturally

The final step denotes a kind of 'mastery learning', the emphasis being on 'doing it naturally', conveying the internalization of a skill or piece of understanding which is now 'part of oneself'.

The adoption of such a system implies the development of shared meanings of each of the categories, as would be the case for the following categorization which comes from the study of Scottish Schools by Black *et al*, where a five-point scale is suggested:

1. Indicates that the child has great difficulty and needs much individual teaching (perhaps from a teacher of learning difficulties).
2. Indicates that the child has had some difficulty but is progressing with extra help from the teacher.
3. Indicates that progress is satisfactory — the child can do/understand what is asked of him.
4. Indicates that the child copes easily with the tasks given him.
5. Indicates that the child has absolutely no problem and is able to work on his own with minimum assistance from the teacher. Obviously, few children fall into this category. (Black *et al*, 1989)

Another example of employing a set of developmental criteria to monitor and record children's progress is illustrated in the Project Assessment Sheet adapted by the Isle of Wight from the Schools Council Project, *Developing Children's Thinking through Topic Work*.

Figure 6.4: Recording by Rating Scale

Project Assessment for .... An Individual Record Sheet based on one of many models described in the SCDC Topic Work Resource Bank. NB: Please leave empty any box relating to a skill which the child has no experience of	Child cannot do this at all	Child has some capability – with help	Child has some capability – independently	Child appears to have mastered this skill
A: The Personal Choice of A Topic	1	2	3	4
Does he spontaneously ask questions about things/people/events around him?				
Does he persist in asking questions until he is satisfied with the answers?				
Can he decide on a topic that he wants to pursue?				
B: The Planning of the Project				
Does he know what fields of knowledge are relevant to his chosen topics?				
Can he decide what questions he wants to ask, and thus what information to look for?				
Can he decide what sources of information he is going to use?				
C: The Selection of Sources Relevant to the Project				
Does he know that information and ideas can be obtained from people, books, the classroom, the wider environment?				
Can he decide which of these sources might be relevant to his project?				
Can he identify information relevant to his project from a variety of sources?				
D: The Extraction of Relevant Information from the Sources				
Can he formulate a sequence of questions to obtain the information that he wants?				
Can he read with understanding, recognizing information relevant to his questions?				
Is he acquiring some of the following:				
Bookskills – using a table of contents				
– using an index				
– using a catalogue				
– using the library/research centre				
Observation skills – Listening				
– Watching				
Reading skills – Scanning				
– Summarizing				
– Note-taking				
Survey and/or questionnaire techniques				

E: The Organization of Information Relevant to the Project

Can he express information and ideas in an appropriate sequence in whatever medium he is using, e.g. speech, drama, writing, pictures?				
Can he relate information he has acquired to the question(s) he has asked?				
Can he link together the different parts of the project and organise the information and ideas he has acquired in a suitably clear and precise way?				
Is he acquiring some of the following:				

– Classifying
    – Ordering
    – Analysing
    – Synthesizing				

F: The Selection of Appropriate Ways of Expressing Information and Ideas

Does he know that information and ideas can be expressed in a variety of ways?				
Is he acquiring some of the following skills:				
– Painting				
– Model-making				
– Writing				
– Sketching				
– Map-making				
– Tape-recording				
– Drawing diagrams				
– Discussion				
– Debating				
– Verbal reporting				
Can he select a form of expression which most clearly conveys his information and ideas in relation to his questions using some of the above skills?				

G: The Self-Evaluation of the Project

Can he judge how adequate his project is in relation to the question(s) he has asked?				
Does he recognize an improvement in the skills he is using?				
Can he assess his approach, presentation and the general quality of his work?				
Can he assess the criticisms of others?				

H: The Self-Motivation to Carry Out and Complete the Project in Accordance with the Plans Made

Are his skills adequate for what he wants to do?				
Can he set criteria for his own achievement and assess it?				
Does he value his achievements?				

(Isle of Wight, 1988)

Recording by Continua

An alternative to recording by ticks or on a rating scale is to employ the use of a continuum. An example to illustrate this come from Wynne Harlen's *Match and Mismatch*. Recordings of children's responses occur over time and provide an indication of progress.

Figure 6.5: Recording by Continua

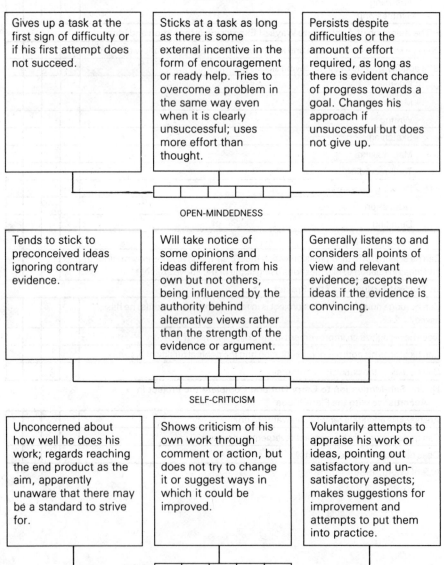

PERSEVERANCE

| Gives up a task at the first sign of difficulty or if his first attempt does not succeed. | Sticks at a task as long as there is some external incentive in the form of encouragement or ready help. Tries to overcome a problem in the same way even when it is clearly unsuccessful; uses more effort than thought. | Persists despite difficulties or the amount of effort required, as long as there is evident chance of progress towards a goal. Changes his approach if unsuccessful but does not give up. |

OPEN-MINDEDNESS

| Tends to stick to preconceived ideas ignoring contrary evidence. | Will take notice of some opinions and ideas different from his own but not others, being influenced by the authority behind alternative views rather than the strength of the evidence or argument. | Generally listens to and considers all points of view and relevant evidence; accepts new ideas if the evidence is convincing. |

SELF-CRITICISM

| Unconcerned about how well he does his work; regards reaching the end product as the aim, apparently unaware that there may be a standard to strive for. | Shows criticism of his own work through comment or action, but does not try to change it or suggest ways in which it could be improved. | Voluntarily attempts to appraise his work or ideas, pointing out satisfactory and un-satisfactory aspects; makes suggestions for improvement and attempts to put them into practice. |

RESPONSIBILITY

Seems unaware of what his role should be, or neglects his part, in activities such as routines, clearing up or getting on with work without constant supervision.	Carries out tasks which are expected of him in response to rules or direction but may neglect tasks in the absence of incentives or external constraints.	Fulfils his role in getting on with the work and carrying out tasks expected of him to the best of his ability without constant supervision. Attempts to overcome problems for himself before asking for help.

INDEPENDENCE

Tends to accept anything he is told by others without question. Makes decisions or forms ideas based only on what others do or say.	Very tentative about deciding things for himself in a new situation but more confident in familiar situations; rather more willing to change his ideas than to defend them if others disagree.	Makes up his mind about what to do or think after considering the available evidence or alternatives and is prepared to defend his opinions or ideas and not change them just to be in line with others.

OBSERVING

Makes limited use of his senses, noticing only some of the things which can be observed in the situation or only those which are pointed out.	Makes all kinds of observations, using several senses, though not able to discriminate the more important from the less important observations for the enquiry in hand.	Makes wide-ranging observations and can select from them the information relevant to a particular problem or enquiry.

Figure 6.5: continued

The matrix completed over time may look something like this:

Autumn 1973 ▨

Summer 1974 ▨

Observing

Raising questions

Exploring

Problem solving

Finding patterns

Communicating verbally

Communicating non-verbally

Applying learning

Concept of causality

Concept of time

Concept of weight

Concept of length

Concept of area

Concept of volume

Classification

Curiosity

Originality

Perseverance etc....

(Harlen *et al.*, 1977)

Recording Progress through 'Shorthand' Procedures

A variety of diagrammatic procedures have been developed to ease the process of recording children's progress, as is illustrated by the two following examples. The first comes from a study of assessment in Scottish primary schools and the second from a topic-recording system included in the Isle of Wight's publication, *Topic Work How and Why?* As was suggested in Chapter 3, however, the major issue with such procedures is concerned with ensuring that each category is reliably interpreted, i.e. that each teacher interprets it in the same way every time it is used. We can only be sure of this if the process is kept under regular review, which is the case for all of the procedures described.

Figure 6.6: Recording by Diagrams

A record of pupil progress in mathematics

Pupils	Topics	1	2	3	4	5	6	7	8
Nov 30	J Aitken	✓	✓	✓	△	✓	△	✓	✓
	M Duncan	✓	✓	✓	✓	✓	△	△	✓
	R Laidlaw	✓	✓	✓	✓	✓	△	✓	✓
Jan 6	R Baird	✓	✓	△	✓	✓	□	△	✓
	C Deans	✓	✓	✓	△	✓	□	□	✓
	G Hastings	✓	✓	△	✓	✓	□	△	✓
	D White	✓	✓	✓	△	✓	△	□	△

✓ = topic mastered
△ = needs more practise
□ = this requires re-teaching –
concept not understood – nothing to build on

(Black *et al.*, 1989)

Figure 6.7: Recording by Diagrams

Topic Record (as used in the Topic 'Our School')

Concepts, ideas and skills children have been exposed to: /
Concepts, ideas and skills children have used: ∠
Concepts, ideas and skills children have mastered: △

This key makes on-the-spot recording quick and easy, as different aspects of a topic are completed. Having all the children's names on one page avoids turning a page for each child, while space left for an end-of-term summary gives easy reference when writing reports.

/ will be written for all children who have been present when the work/experience took place.

∠ indicates successful practice, while △ will only be completed when understanding, assimilation and application have been proven.

Two additions which may be found useful are ? denoting an area of difficulty, or * for special aptitude. By placing a ruler under a child's horizontal record, the pattern of development is readily seen. The numbers are directly cross-referenced to the objectives of the particular schools, in this case 1–10, so that the teacher can monitor the way in which a topic is providing scope for meeting the agreed aims. Where it is not, as in the example provided, other opportunities must be provided in areas not being adequately covered.

The value of such record-keeping is that it is made at the time and this builds up throughout the term, based on direct evidence rather than relying on teacher's memory in end-of-term form-filling. Rather than recording only the maths/reading/writing subjects, all areas of knowledge and experience can be included. Children perceive the teacher taking as much interest in testing a model, discussing a painting, or dramatic

115

interpretation, so that every child is more likely to achieve success in some sphere. These record sheets can be passed to subsequent teachers who can quickly scan the subject matter covered, to ensure progression, building on previous experience, and avoiding unnecessary repetition of content. It also highlights children's absences in specific areas, which may account for later problems where no compensatory action has been taken. Conversely, by not having a previous teacher's assessment on the same page, the child is more likely to receive a fresh review of his potential, free from the self-perpetuating bias of some grading systems.

Week ending	Making a Pond Identifying Pond Life	Written Description 'Where we Live'	Tree Identification Drawing/Labelling	Teaching younger children	Map making	Diary Write/Read	Wild Flowers Identification
	12 Sep	12 Sep	12 Sep	19 Sep	19 Sep	19 Sep	19 Sep
Curriculum Objectives Ref.	1 2 3 4 ⑤ ⑥ 7 8⑨ 10	1② 3 4 ⑤ 6 7 8 9 10	1 ② ③ 4 ⑤ 6 7 8 9 10	① 2 ③ 4 5 6 7 8 9 ⑩	1 2 3 ④ ⑤ 6 7 8 9 10	1 ② 3 4 ⑤ 6 7 8 9 10	1 ② ③ 4 ⑤ 6 7 8 9 10
Matthew 8 y	∠	△	△	∠	/	∠	∠
Kelly 7 y 10 m	△	∠	∠	∠	△	△	∠
Anne 7 y 7 m	∠	a	/	∠	∠	/	∠

(Isle of Wight, 1988)

Recording National Curriculum Assessments

With the advent of the National Curriculum and statutory requirements to report to parents, a number of examples of how this might be undertaken are beginning to emerge. The SISTA classroom record (Summative Informal System for Teacher Assessment) has been developed by Professor Michael Bassey at Trent Polytechnic. The SISTA provides an end-of-the-school-year report for parents in terms of the number of statements of attainment which a child is judged to have achieved in each profile component of the foundation subjects. The example which follows illustrates the reporting procedure for children at Key stage one.

Most recent developments in recording and reporting have been associated with Profiling and Records of Achievement. Initially aimed at secondary schools, the purposes of *Records of Achievement* as outlined by the Department of Education and Science were:

Figure 6.8: Recording National Curriculum Assessments

SISTA RECORD FOR REPORTING TO PARENTS   Name ....

This report gives the school's assessment of your child's progress by the end of the school year in the National Curriculum in English, Mathematics and Science. Key Stage One of the National Curriculum at present contains 228 Statements of Attainment and the first column shows the number at each Level in each component. The second and third columns show the number of Statements of Attainment which your child is assessed as having achieved by the end of Year One and Year Two.

		Total number of NC statements	Record at end of Year One	Record at end of Year Two
ENGLISH Speaking and listening	Level 1	3	☐	☐
	Level 2	5	☐	☐
	Level 3	4	☐	☐
ENGLISH Reading	Level 1	4	☐	☐
	Level 2	6	☐	☐
	Level 3	6	☐	☐
ENGLISH Writing	Level 1	5	☐	☐
	Level 2	10	☐	☐
	Level 3	10	☐	☐
MATHEMATICS Component One	Level 1	9	☐	☐
	Level 2	15	☐	☐
	Level 3	18	☐	☐
MATHEMATICS Component Two	Level 1	11	☐	☐
	Level 2	13	☐	☐
	Level 3	13	☐	☐
SCIENCE Exploration	Level 1	2	☐	☐
	Level 2	6	☐	☐
	Level 3	9	☐	☐
SCIENCE Knowledge	Level 1	18	☐	☐
	Level 2	30	☐	☐
	Level 3	31	☐	☐

(Trent Assessment Guide for Primary Schools, 1990)

— to recognize achievement, acknowledging and giving credit for what children have experienced and achieved, not just through assessment procedures, but in other ways as well;

— that a record of achievement should contribute to personal development and increase motivation and self-awareness, provide encouragement and increase awareness of strengths, weaknesses and opportunities;

— that it should encourage a review of curriculum and organization, to consider how well the curriculum, teaching and school organization enable children to develop general, practical and social skills;

— that it should provide a document of record, recognized and valued, consisting of a short summary document giving a record of achievement which presents a more 'rounded' picture of each individual. (DES, 1984/1990)

All of these principles seem perfectly appropriate to the practice of reporting and recording primary school pupils' progress, and a number of writers have commented upon and offered examples to illustrate how this might be enacted in primary schools (Inkson, 1987; Black, 1989; DES, 1990).

More recently, the DES invited Essex to undertake a pilot study of records of achievement in primary schools which focused upon three main areas:

the process of recording achievement;
reporting to parents;
the nature of the report. (Essex LEA, 1990)

The project examined practice in thirteen schools in the authority as well as elsewhere, and concluded that there was a great deal of practice in primary schools which fulfilled the criteria of records of achievement, and that they offered a useful means of conveying the whole range of a child's competence, including National Curriculum achievements. As a result of the study they offered a number of recommendations, suggesting that:

the recording of achievement should reflect the individuality of each school and avoid formally prescribed models;

any report should include common elements, notably some form of personal record maintained by the child of achievements in and out of school;

each child should be actively involved in the process of assessment and recording, selecting work and as a participant in a review with parent(s) and teacher(s);

with regard to the requirements of the Education Reform Act, it was felt that a written report required by statutory legislation should be seen as one part of a process of consultation. Reports should be seen as written agreed statements between parent, teacher and child. The content should include comments on relationships, attitudes and non-curricular achievements as well as curriculum-based achievements;

the written report should be informative and motivating, user-friendly and jargon-free, positive and encouraging;

in the record of achievement, four sections were suggested: a record of school experiences; a personal record by the child; a record of curriculum progress in relation to National Curriculum achievements; and a representative sample of work chosen in consultation with the child.

Whatever the procedure adopted in developing recording systems, there are a number of important basic principles that need to be adhered to. The Schools Council Project concluded, somewhat obviously, that records should have:

a clear layout;
clear stable printing that will not fade;
clear section headings;
the pupil's name in a prominent position (usually top right-hand corner);
sufficient space provided for comments;
a prominently placed key or users' handbook to explain the use of abbreviations, symbols and criteria for the assessment of pupils.

Record content should:

be relevant to the purpose of the record;
be clearly sequenced;
give direct indications for future teaching rather than implications;
give a clear distinction between entries concerned with pupils' school experiences and those which are assessments of attainment;
clearly present assessment information stating
(a) the derivation of norms used when grading or rating
(b) the criteria used when deciding on a pupil's competence
(c) details of standardized tests used as a basis for grading or rating
(d) details of other testing techniques used
(e) teacher-made test marks in a standardized form to indicate the range and distribution of scores. This is particularly important where sets of marks from different sources have to be compared.

More recently, the National Curriculum council has suggested that any record keeping system should include:

a clear and agreed definition of terms;
an agreement about the function of records;
clearly and coherently presented records;
carefully considered storage;
previously agreed and understood access;
recognized confidentiality;

efficient and time-effective methods;
pupils as a part of the process, where appropriate;
recorded outcomes as a result of parental discussion.

(NCC, 1989)

A recent discussion paper on assessment by the Geographical Association asked some important questions about recording:

1. Why record? (It is important to be clear about the purposes of any record-keeping activity.)
2. Who is the record for? (This will determine the kind of record required.)
3. What is to be recorded? (It is impossible to record everything; sort it out before starting.)
4. When do you record? (When records are made is likely to affect their quality.)
5. How often do you record? (The frequency of recording will have an impact on the quality.)
6. How many records do you keep? (It is important to avoid duplication.)
7. Who do you keep records on? (Individuals, classes, year groups, key stages.)
8. Where should they be kept? (It is important to think about storage.)
9. How are they organized? What system is to be used?
10. How much evidence is kept, and of what kind?
11. Who has access to the record?
12. Do you need to assess and record achievement for every activity? (No! planning is essential.)
13. How is recording to be consistent? (Lambert, 1990)

Drummond offers some other important issues to consider when evaluating existing systems or preparing new reporting systems:

Is there variety in the information-collecting procedures (see Chapter 4 for examples) to validate judgements?

Is the system an active one, stimulating further enquiry, rather than a static system reporting the end of the process?

Does the system reflect the values of the school as a whole, and is it based on shared and agreed meanings?

Does it record change and progress?

Does it focus upon achievement — what children *can* do rather than what they cannot do?

Is it accessible to parents?

Is it used by teachers and the school as part of their review process? Is it checked to see if it is working? If not, change it! (Drummond, 1989)

This final comment leads into the next chapter, which argues that in order to cope with the demands of assessment it is essential to work towards establishing an assessment policy for the whole school.

Chapter 7

Towards a Policy for Assessment

The National Curriculum Council has suggested that one of the ways in which schools can cope with the demands of the National Curriculum is to produce a School Development Plan, and that a central feature of this should be 'a whole-school policy on assessment and record-keeping'.

Such a policy would include:

a clear indication of what assessment is;
why we undertake assessment;
how we assess;
how we record those assessments;
how we communicate those assessments;
the procedures adopted to keep the whole process under review;

so that assessments continue to be a central feature of the teaching and learning processes in our schools.

The Task Group on Assessment and Testing believes that:

(3) Promoting children's learning is a principal aim of schools. Assessment lies at the heart of this process. It can provide a framework within which educational objectives may be set and pupils' progress charted and expressed. It can yield a basis for planning the next educational steps in response to children's needs. By facilitating dialogue between teachers, it can enhance professional skills and help the school as a whole to strengthen learning across the curriculum and through its age range.
(4) The assessment process itself should not determine what is to be taught and learned. It should be the servant, not the master, of the curriculum. Yet it should not simply be a bolt-on addition at the end... It therefore needs to be incorporated systematically into teaching strategies at all levels. (DES, 1988)

This chapter will attempt to provide an overview of the development of an assessment policy. A variety of authors has advocated the importance of seizing the initiative on assessment. Ruth Sutton (1990) suggests that there is a strong temptation to do absolutely nothing until the goalposts stop moving, but advocates that some preparation is both sensible and necessary. This is best undertaken, she suggests, as a whole school, not only to reduce the demands on teachers, but also to be realistic about the implications for children.

> A whole-school framework is absolutely essential. Only through teamwork will teachers find the confidence not to be overzealous in demands they place upon children. (Lambert, 1990)

This is a view endorsed by Holly and Southworth in the introductory text to this series. A developing or thinking school is one in which there is a recognition of the existence of multiple perspectives and space for each person's point of view to be valued, yet at the same time a recognition that some compromise has to be achieved by the whole staff group. This implies:

> ... teacher-participation in the school as a learning, inquiring, problem-solving system. Teacher commitment to, and co-ownership of, the developmental learning process is a cornerstone of school-based development. (Holly, 1989)

Ainscow and Conner have argued, however, that:

> Some teachers are more aware of the importance of their own professional development than others. They approach their work with a questioning frame of mind, seeking to explore new possibilities and find ways of teaching that will be an improvement on their current practice. Equally, some schools are better than others at creating an atmosphere for professional development.
>
> In considering ways of developing policy and/or practice, therefore, the existing attitudes of individuals and the pervading atmosphere within a school are important factors. (Ainscow and Conner, 1990)

Michael Fullan has suggested that the introduction of any innovation is threatening and that successful adoption and implementation of new ideas requires that people understand the purpose and meanings associated with changing practice. He also reminds us that such change is really about learning new ways of thinking and behaving:

> ... successful change, successful implementation, is none other than learning, only it is the adults in the situation who are learning, more so than the pupils. (Fullan, 1982)

This means that the school should be seen as a place where teachers learn from their experience in the same way that they hope their children learn from the tasks and activities in which they are engaged. Schools, Holly argues (1990) need to be schools for learning as opposed to schools for teaching.

The introduction of significant changes involving the adoption of new ways of thinking and different ways of operating in the classroom should also be seen as a process, not an event. Fullan argues that fundamental ideas do not change at a particular moment in time, but via a gradual process of assimilation and modification of existing ideas and practice, which occur over time. Evidence from social psychologists suggests that for complex organizations like schools to adopt new ways of working can take from three to five years. Yet so often in school the time-scale for the introduction of ideas is too short, and we often make things worse by trying to do too many things at the same time. It is also important to remember that the development and introduction of a new policy can often be an untidy and uncomfortable experience.

> As individuals seek to relate new ideas and ways of working to their own unique range of personal experiences, preferences and prejudices, they can become distorted, adapted or, indeed, totally converted into a form that is more acceptable. Consequently, the original purpose, despite having been presented in a logical and rational form, may come to mean something quite different as a result of its own adoption by other people. (Ainscow and Conner, 1990)

With regard to assessment, it provides an opportunity to influence the process of future events if we are able to seize the initiative, and, as has been suggested earlier (Chapter 4), developing our assessment skills can improve our understanding of the nature of the learning process. Teacher-assessment, properly developed, could become a central feature of the National Curriculum, and by implication provide teachers with an opportunity to influence the direction of future developments. Blyth has stated:

> The arguments in favour of assessment ... should warrant the development of a positive policy in each school, whether or not there is any kind of national curriculum ... That does not mean that a school's policy should be confined to implementing what will be the legal minimum. There will be plenty of scope for schools to go beyond that minimum and to develop their own strategies in a constructive and creative way ... and will empower

schools, working as they must within the new framework, to seize the essential initiative. (Blyth, 1990)

It is important we do seize the initiative, for as Lambert suggests, 'Come what may, teacher-assessment will always be an important part of our professional lives'.

A recent discussion on assessment by Hargreaves identifies four main intentions underlying current thinking about assessment:

> that there needs to be an improvement in the quality of teachers' marking, recording and assessing;
>
> that improving teachers' skills of assessment enhances the quality of pupils' learning;
>
> that parents should be given regular information about their children's achievements, including performance relative to their peers;
>
> that parents are entitled to more information about the quality of the school, including performance relative to those in other schools.

Most teachers, he argues, are comfortable with the first two expectations but less comfortable with the last two. He suggests that those in Government appear to believe that if the last propositions can be brought into effect, the first two will naturally occur. At present, he suggests, this is hypothetical:

> Providing parents with information about a child's relative achievement (e.g. position in class) or about the school's overall relative performance (e.g. 11-plus or examination results) has not in the past led inexorably to improved assessment or achievement, so why should the new forms of assessment do so in the age of the National Curriculum? (Hargreaves, 1990)

He believes that we need to be clearer about what we support and accept as far as assessment in education is concerned. In addition to the four listed above he offers the following, all of which have been advocated in this book:

> pupils' learning improves when assessment is diagnostic of their difficulties;
>
> pupils' learning improves when they engage in self-diagnosis and self-assessment;
>
> simple quantified statements of achievement are sometimes desirable, but, because of dangers of crude labelling and under-expectation, should be kept to a minimum;
>
> giving parents information on pupils' achievements is only one aspect of a school's accountability;
>
> assessment of pupils should always take far less time than teaching;
>
> pupils' learning is enhanced through a close partnership between

teachers and parents rather than through a model of accountability derived from commercialism;

an assessment policy which enhances pupils' learning should not '... unthinkingly indulge the English obsession with the grading, ranking, rating, sorting and classifying of pupils by test results'.

Developing a Policy

Given that we all start from different positions in our understanding, views and beliefs about assessment, the first requirement in developing a school policy is to explore the different perspectives of the group. The activities offered at the end of Chapter 1 are a useful starting point for these discussions. They can be further explored by engaging in a diamond ranking activity exploring reactions to the views of others about assessment. For this task, colleagues are invited to consider nine different statements about assessment in small groups and arrange them in an order which they can explain, support and justify, e.g.

1

2   2

3   3   3

4   4

5

When the groups have completed this task they should be invited to combine groups and explain their diamond rank. This is not just a process of comparison, but requires justification. The listening group acts as a critical audience posing questions to test their presenter's justifications. Some exemplar statements for this activity are included in Appendix B.

Following on from an activity of this kind, it is a natural process to begin to identify some principles for assessment to guide the production of a policy statement. The Geographical Association has engaged in such a process and has identified the following as important basic principles for a policy for assessment:

Assessment must be integral to teaching.

Assessment must be enjoyable.

Assessment must provide all students with the opportunity to demonstrate achievement and attainment, irrespective of ability, gender, race, or special educational need.

Assessment should involve the pupil; for example, clear assessment objectives can be shared with the pupil.

Assessment should involve the pupil by providing the opportunity to review his/her progress and assessment results.

Assessment should involve the pupil in target-setting as the basis of assessments.

A variety of techniques should be employed so that assessment is fit for the purpose.

Assessment strategies should be agreed by all teachers involved in the assessment.

The opportunity should be available to assess when ready and reassess if necessary.

Assessment techniques should be chosen that are appropriate to the needs of the pupils; not of the teachers. A variety of assessment techniques can be used with different pupils to assess the same objective.

Another example of an attempt to provide a checklist for the development of a policy comes from Black *et al.* (1989). As they comment, it is not intended as a blueprint to be followed slavishly, but can serve as a useful starting point for discussion. Any assessment policy should include:

1. An account of the ways in which assessment will be used to fulfil different purposes, e.g. diagnosis and monitoring.
2. A description of the relationship between assessment, forward planning and teaching.
3. Details of matters (set in the context of different areas of the curriculum) such as the forms of assessment to use, timing of assessment, recording and storing of information.
4. Details of how consistency within the school will be achieved (interpretation of grades, codes, etc).
5. Details of how reporting to parents is organized.
6. Details of information to be transferred to
   (a) next year's teacher
   (b) the associated secondary school.
7. Details of responsibilities of individual staff members in relation to assessment.
8. Arrangements for evaluating and reviewing the policy.

In addition to the identification of basic principles of an assessment policy, it is also important to remember that there are some essential characteristics about assessment that have to be borne in mind. Underpinning any framework for assessment are three fundamental technical issues:

> fitness for purpose
> validity;
> reliability.

Fitness for Purpose, Validity and Reliability

There is a great variety of assessment procedures, strategies and techniques available for us to use, ranging from formal standardized tasks to informal teacher-structured activities, including those requiring a written response, a diagrammatic representation or some kind of behavioural evidence. Different methods are appropriate to different circumstances. We need to develop skills in the appropriate selection of tasks to suit the assessment intended. A corollary of this is that decisions about assessment need to be central to our planning and embedded within it. The example that follows on page 130 is an example of an attempt to consider the means of assessment suitable to a particular subject area.

The second technical issue, *validity*, leads us to ask the question, 'Are we assessing what we think we are assessing?'. An assessment with high validity is one which gets as close as possible to the children's understanding: to what the learner knows, understands and can do. *Reliability* is concerned with the extent to which the results can be relied upon.

> To achieve 'reliable' assessment you try to reduce the main variables which can affect the judgement. There are three major variables in most assessment by teachers: context (the circumstances of assessment); time (how many times and over what period of time you have to see an assessment criterion achieved); and 'rater' (that is, the person doing the assessment). To put if briefly, do what you can to agree with your colleagues how you can reduce these variables ... Assessment is an art, not a science, and much of the time you will be relying on your professional judgement and common sense, employing more stringent techniques only when you're in doubt. (Sutton, 1990)

For each assessment activity, therefore, it is necessary to plan ahead bearing in mind a number of further important questions in the development of policy.

Which technique is most appropriate?

Figure 7.1: Embedding Assessment into Planning

PUPIL'S NAME: .... SESSION: .... CLASS: ....

EVIDENCE CURRIC-AREA	WRITTEN	ORAL	OBSERVATION
LANGUAGE	Review jotters, workbooks and worksheets. Mention written expression; written responses to comprehension; presentation; vocabulary.	Mainly based on impressions formed from group and class discussions. Fluency; confidence; willingness to contribute; oral reading.	Based generally on impressions on how day-to-day work is carried out – enthusiasm; commitment; application etc. Reading ability.
MATHEMATICS	Review as above: consistency; accuracy; presentation; special areas of difficulty.	As above.	As above, but also: retention; ability with mental arithmetic; practical maths problem-solving.
ENVIRONMENTAL STUDIES	Based on project folders, jotters etc. Presentation: ability to complete set tasks; independent reference work – quantity and quality.	As above. Level of interest. Questioning. General knowledge.	As for language. Also involvement and ability with science assignments.
EXPRESSIVE ARTS	Based on general impressions of day-to-day work and also in the case of art and craft on quality of end results. Level of enjoyment in each aspect.		
RELIGIOUS EDUCATION	Based mainly on observations during discussions and lessons; also quality of written work/art work, etc.		
RECREATIONAL ACTIVITIES	From informal observations and interactions; e.g. if keen recreational reader, etc., or from direct questioning as to hobbies, etc.		
TESTS	Enter results of e.g. Edinburgh Reading Tests; Quest Tests; Spelling Tests.		
ATTITUDES	General comments on general levels of concentration: efforts; application and the likes.		

(Black *et al.*, 1989)

What is the simplest and most useful means of recording?

What evidence of learning is the activity likely to generate?

How can I be sure that my interpretation is valid and reliable?

How will I manage the classroom to enable the assessment to take place?

Given these starting points for the development of a school policy, the following examples might be used to start discussion, or as a comparison with something produced within your school. It is also possible to compare the principles highlighted at the beginning of this chapter with the proposals described, and consider how far the assessment principles have been subscribed to. The first example comes from the London Borough of Hillingdon's Assessment advice to teachers; the second from Hertfordshire's advice on assessment; and the third, from Suffolk, offers some useful questions associated with the process of policy development.

The next chapter goes on to consider how one local authority and one primary school have attempted to put ideas discussed here into practice.

Assessment Policies: 1

1. We see the three most important aims of the process of assessment as being:
   (i) diagnostic — to help pupils learn
   (ii) to help us to evaluate the effectiveness of our own teaching
   (iii) to provide information for a third party, the most obvious examples being parents and potential employers.
2. The process of assessment should arise out of, and be determined by, the nature of the curriculum. It is important that a balance be maintained between the three main elements in the educative process: curriculum — pedagogy — assessment.
3. The main emphasis in all forms of assessment should be on the recognition and acknowledgement of pupil-achievement.
4. We see it as essential that pupils should have some involvement in the assessment of their own efforts as a means towards increasing the effectiveness of their learning. The generation of more active learning roles for pupils is the most likely way to improve understanding.
5. With many forms of assessment it is the process of assessment, rather than the assessment outcome, which is its most valuable feature. Wherever possible, assessment should offer pointers to the future. Too much assessment has been concerned with the recording of information which is little or never used.

6. Assessment should enable pupils to measure themselves more effectively against the needs and demands of the course they are studying — not against the performance of other pupils.
7. Wherever possible the nature, aims and main content areas of a course should be made known to pupils at the outset as a means of extending their awareness of their own educational development and involvement in their progress. (London Borough of Hillingdon, 1989: Assessment INSET)

Assessment Policies: 2

PRINCIPLES OF ASSESSMENT

1. Assessment is an integral and helpful part of the teaching and learning process, and facilitates the essential task of matching curriculum to attainment and ability.
2. Methods of assessment should be consistent with our understanding of how children best learn, and supporting that learning.
3. Forms of agreement should be manageable, coherent, systematic, valid, sufficient and appropriate for the intended purposes and meaningful to all users.
4. Assessment of a child's learning should include the full range of learning activities with which s/he is engaged. These include not only the assessment of National Curriculum attainment targets, but the development of attitudes, etc.
5. Assessment must take account of the wide range of individual needs including those associated with mother tongues* and cultural background.
6. Assessment should be based on criteria which are explicit and capable of being readily understood by pupils, teachers, parents and others.
7. All pupils are entitled to a formative record of progress across the broadest span of achievement, within and beyond the National Curriculum and including areas of achievement identified by the pupil.
8. Recording of assessment should emphasize achievement.

---

*The Assessment of bilingual pupils who are at an early stage in their learning of English should be mother tongue.
Assessment should be free from gender bias. (Hewett and Bennett, 1989)

9. Opportunities should be found for pupil self-assessment to foster self-awareness and encourage greater responsibility for learning.
10. Constructive, positive and regular discussion between teacher and pupil to review progress and identify strengths and weaknesses will help inform agreements on future learning targets. This process will be informed by regular discussion with parents.
11. All the processes of formative assessment and record keeping will be the basis for the production of a summative report.

Developing a whole-school policy for assessment

Ten-point plan involving policy and practice

Identify an assessment co-ordinator;
Establish a commitment to the use of formative assessment;
Ensure that assessment opportunities are built into the curriculum;
Identify curriculum opportunities which enable pupils to demonstrate their best achievements;
Establish procedures for review and evaluation;
Agree ways of recording pupils' curriculum opportunities and their achievements against statements of attainment;
Generate criteria and develop procedures for selecting and keeping samples of pupils' work;
Arrange for regular agreement trials and other moderation procedures;
Consider storage of and access to records;
Decide on how best to report to parents, and transfer and receive records at end of year/key stage. (Suffolk LEA, 1989)

Chapter 8

Case Studies of Assessment in Action

Reaction to the demands of the National Curriculum and its assessment resulted in an immense amount of activity in Local Authorities throughout the country. Evidence suggests that an enormous amount of energy was invested in this and there was a certain amount of reinventing the wheel. Participation in local authority working parties, cluster groups and school-based discussion about assessment has certainly proved a worthwhile experience for many teachers, however, and has contributed significantly to their own thinking and personal development. The two case studies presented in this chapter represent two levels of policy-making. The first is by Margaret Evans, an advisory teacher with responsibility for coordinating in-service on assessment for primary teachers within the large Local Education Authority of Essex. The second contribution comes from Stephen Benyon, the headteacher of a primary school within that authority, and describes his attempts to structure a policy for his school based upon the advice offered within his LEA. The Chief Education Officer for Essex was a member of the Task Group on Assessment and Testing and elected to be pro-active with regard to developing assessment within his LEA. As a result, twenty primary and twenty secondary teachers were seconded for one day a week to explore assessment practice both within and beyond the authority with a view to offering advice by teachers for teachers.

Margaret coordinated the primary group and Stephen was one of the seconded teachers who worked on the project.

Case Study 1

*A Personal Perspective on One Local Authority's INSET
Programme in Preparation for Assessment (Margaret Evans)*

On appointment as advisory teacher for assessment in primary schools, my
main task was to coordinate the production of a set of assessment materials to
be written by a team of twenty primary and special school teachers. At all
times it was appreciated that the material was being written by teachers, for
teachers, and before any National Curriculum documentation was available
to us. It was intended from the outset that the material would be reviewed
and revised to reflect national developments in the subsequent academic
year. In exactly the same way, a team of secondary and special school teachers
was also formed to produce suitable material for their colleagues. We all felt
that, ideally, one set of materials should have been produced, but agreed
that our objective was to support our colleagues, and clearly we were writing
for different audiences with different needs at that time. My colleague,
Richard Roberts, took overall responsibility for the Secondary material, and
in fact was involved in starting off the project for both teams before my
appointment. The Authority felt that, with a total of approximately 750
schools, and the need to introduce some of the issues concerned with the
implementation of the National Curriculum and assessment beginning in
September 1989, distance-learning materials would offer one means of
support to all teachers and to the School Assessment Leader (SAL). This was
to be backed up by a training programme throughout the county. To the
members of the team this became known as 'Bob's Vision', as it was the
creation and far-sightedness of a comprehensive programme envisaged by
our County Inspector for Assessment and Examinations, Mr R. G. E. Wood.
A diagram of this programme appears in Figure 8.1.

The intention was that the teachers who had produced the material (or
the Assessment Training Workshop [ATW]) would be available to support
teachers in school, as requested, because they could be released from their
own schools for one day per week throughout the Summer term 1989. School
Assessment Leader training days were held during the Spring term 1989, and
on those days we hoped to offer colleagues the opportunity to express their
concerns and to be informed of the support material which would be coming
into schools, both in the form of the materials themselves and the
availability of the Assessment Training Workshop team members.

Prior to my appointment, Richard had organized a residential course
for the primary group, and many speakers — advisory teachers and
inspectors from the LEA, HMI, lecturers from the Anglia and Cambridge
Institutes and other visitors — helped to shape the thinking of the

Figure 8.1: Assessment Training Support Programme

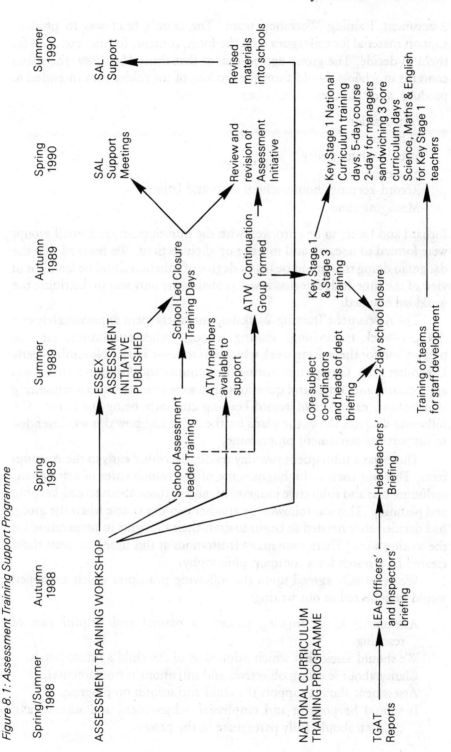

Assessment Training Workshop team. The team's brief was to produce support material for colleagues, and the form, content, format, etc., was for them to decide. The group agreed that at that time, May 1989, the major concerns in schools should form the sections of the folder they intended to produce, and that these should be:

Introduction
Why assess?
Whole-school policy
Strategies
Record-keeping, home–school links and liaison
Managing time

Richard and I were to be entrusted with the introduction, and small groups were formed to research and to write up their sections. We realized that the danger in doing this would be that a degree of cohesion could be lost, but in view of the time-scale felt that it was probably the only way to distribute the workload entailed.

The Assessment Training Workshop members spent approximately one day per week researching, visiting schools, other authorities, etc., in preparation for the writing week which was to come in late November–early December 1988. Groups met during the Summer and Autumn terms as was appropriate, and letters and questionnaires were sent into school requesting information, examples of record-keeping currently being used, etc. The following diagram shows the plans for the ATW and how this was intended to support the assessment programme.

There was a subsequent two-day residential course early in the Autumn term. This was used to highlight some of the complexities of assessment, including bias and subjective judgement, and to think about record-keeping and planning. This was followed by another two-day course when the group had decided they needed to begin to draft their thoughts in preparation for the writing week. There were many frustrations at this time, not least those created by a search for a common philosophy.

We eventually agreed upon the following principles which we hoped would be reflected in our writing:

Assessment is an ongoing process, a natural and helpful part of teaching.
We should assess that which informs us of the child's future needs.
Clarity about learning objectives and intentions is fundamental.
Assessment should support the child and inform on progress.
It should be positive and emphasize achievement and success, and children should fully participate in the process.

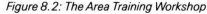

Figure 8.2: The Area Training Workshop

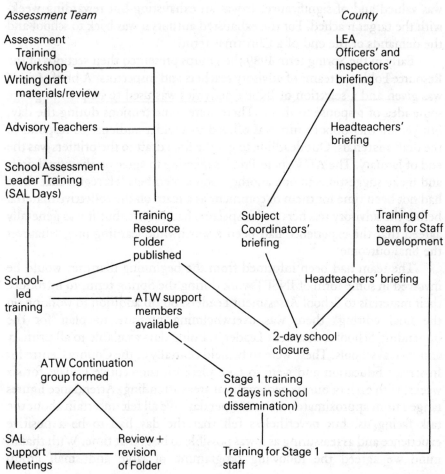

It should be undertaken in a climate where the learner feels valued, and it is by creating this climate that we are likely to encourage the potential in each person to be realized.

The end of November found us assembled in a pleasant hotel in Southend, but the only gulps of bracing sea air that many members of the group were able to gasp were taken on the daily trek from the hotel to the De Havilland Suite which housed our word processors and provided a working base. Everyone worked with purpose and enthusiasm, and the many visitors who arrived could not fail to be impressed by the hard work, determination and group identity engendered by the team. During this time we were visited by our Principal Primary Inspector and other members of the inspectorate, advisory teachers, interested headteachers, etc., and this helped in making the group feel that the work in which they were involved was valued and of significance. It was an exhausting but rewarding week, with the target reached. For the exhausted authors it was back to school and the demands of the end of a Christmas term!

Early in the Spring term 1989 the groups presented their sections of the Resource Folder to teams of advisory teachers and inspectors. A brief résumé was given and a selection of INSET activities was used to help us to gauge some idea of response to them. There were some tensions during the day, but yet another opportunity was offered to a wider audience to respond to the draft materials. Our deadline to get the final draft to the printers was the end of January. The ATW spent Fridays meeting to agree on their final draft and make suggestions to one another. Some members felt regret that there had not been time for them to comment as a team on the collective material before the advisory teachers and inspectors had seen it, but it was generally agreed that the experience had been a worthwhile learning one, whatever the final outcome.

The team had been informed from the beginning that they would be involved in some form of INSET work during the Spring term, to introduce their materials to School Assessment Leaders. So, in addition to working on the final editing, there was overwhelming pressure to plan for the impending School Assessment Leader Training days available to all primary and special schools. These were to be held centrally at the County Centre for In-service Education and were to take place on consecutive Fridays for six weeks, with each of our six geographical areas attending. Attendance figures ranged from approximately 80 to 120 per day. We all felt uncertain about the task facing us, but nevertheless felt that the day had to be a positive experience and as reassuring as it was possible to be at that time. With that in mind we agreed the following programme of large and small group activities.

1. An introduction to the National Curriculum and its assessment and the authority's proposed strategy. (large group)
2. Assessment: What is it? This included some observational activities. (small groups — run by members of the ATW)
3. What will I have to do as a School Assessment Leader? (small groups)
4. What or who will help me? (small groups)
5. What are we doing already? (small groups)
6. Plenary sessions — any questions? (large group)

Our first day received a very mixed reception, and people expressed their anger and frustration because, as a team, we were unable to answer so many of their questions, fears and concerns. The venue we were working in added to the frustration; it was not possible to serve such large numbers of people with coffee, tea, etc., in the time we had allowed. Some people were reassured by the content of the day but, by and large, we all felt a sense of dissatisfaction, and so it was back to the drawing board. We were obliged to keep the content similar as this was a county-wide course, but the team agreed that we needed to rearrange the day to make it more manageable, supportive and practical. A real frustration to many was that we were preparing them for material which was to be available in schools, but was not in their possession at the time. We were able to understand such frustrations, but were convinced that our preparation would be worthwhile, not least in informing colleagues that the Assessment Training Workshop members would be available to support them in their own schools during the Summer term, and to know about the folder before it arrived at school. The day was readjusted and domestic difficulties were overcome by groups taking staggered breaks. We also decided that members of the ATW who were familiar with their own area groups should decide on appropriate local grouping. As the weeks passed we received draft documents and some words of reassurance from SEAC and the DES, and this we were able to incorporate into our day. Visitors from other authorities joined us on occasions and remarked on the positive feeling of each day. As a result of initial experiences we were able to set out the objectives for the day as follows:

1. to have the opportunity to meet members of the Assessment Training Workshop, and to establish contact;
2. to consider the position of assessment within current National Curriculum developments;
3. to be informed of the planned training and support, including the forthcoming resource folder;
4. to have the opportunity to think about the role of the SAL in his/her own school;
5. to begin planning future strategies within your own school and to think about developing a support network; some previously organized networking may well exist.

This modified format was generally better received and was the pattern formed for the remaining courses. The data collected from the course evaluations showed that, despite frustrations created by lack of guidance in assessment and recording on a national level, and also the resource folder not being available on the day, the majority found the day helpful and reassuring and an opportunity to begin to prepare themselves and their staff in some ways for the implementation of the National Curriculum. Some people felt that the day had come too soon, and that it would have been better to wait until more information was available, but time has shown that it is likely that the profession will shape the advice given and we cannot afford to wait to have prescribed orders.

About a third of the way into the course Richard and I decided that it would be helpful to provide the SALs with suggestions for the two-day closure, and also a suggested time-table to support their discussions. We offered the following themes as possible parts of the programme that they would have responsibility for:

> update staff on National Curriculum implementation and terminology;
> curriculum review update (headteacher);
> programmes of study: maths, English, science workshops;
> discuss current assessment practices — discuss Summer term's activity as worked through, possible timetable (below);
> ways forward with classroom assessment recording — records of achievement.

We also suggested that a possible programme of activities in the Summer term 1989 might include the following:

1. Keep things simple. Concentrate on immediate requirements.
2. Pick a topic or theme which has been used, or is being used, to provide focus for discussion.
3. Meet with head, science, maths and English coordinators.
4. Using the topic/theme chosen, let each subject-coordinator see how programmes of study are being met for Key Stage 1.
5. Coordinators to prepare analysis and share their thoughts with one other person (where possible) plus head and SAL (we acknowledged that in many small schools these separate people might not exist).
6. SAL suggests work that staff can identify in their classrooms.
7. Each teacher can look at three levels, in one subject area, spread around their broad age-range, supported by the SAL.
8. Over two weeks teachers can focus on five pupils and assess their level of attainment as a result of their normal teaching.
9. Teachers can feed back their assessment to another teacher plus head /SAL.
10. Teachers could then go on to look at another five pupils to assess their level of attainment in another subject area.
11. They could then begin to review appropriate ways of recording assessments and reporting.
12. SAL could introduce resource folder to staff, preparing them for it and giving people the opportunity to consider how it could be

reviewed, and the contents shared to make dissemination more manageable.

As the weeks passed the content of the days became increasingly well-received, and initial anger and frustration subsided. Visitors from other authorities who joined us wrote to say how helpful and positive they had found the experience. Some course members found the day unhelpful, but generally the analysis of the data indicated a positive response including the comment that the day had been 'excellent'.

During the same term our inspector, Bob Wood, had spoken to all primary headteachers, updating them on the curent situation and introducing them to National Curriculum and assessment terminology and implementation. In the Summer term the ATW were asked to speak to all headteachers on assessment, as this had been identified by them as being one of their major areas of concentration in their curriculum reviews and development plans. These sessions concluded with the following review sheets, which we hoped might offer a useful starting point for reflection in their schools.

Figure 8.3: Assessment Review – Gaining Information

How is work corrected/marked – with or without the children?

Do you want children to understand that assessment is being made? Could this be appropriate?

Are children involved in setting realistic targets for themselves?

Are children encouraged to contribute to open nights/parents' visits, etc.?

Are parents involved in the assessment of/planning for the child?

Are reports made? If so, when and in what kind of ways?

Are negative comments accepted in reporting?

Are skills, attitudes, social and physical development, etc., included?

Do children contribute in any way towards the reporting?

Do children and teachers discuss and plan work?

Are achievements emphasized?

Do planning steps meet individual needs and are they clear?

Are the children involved in any form of self-assessment?

Is assessment designed to motivate?

Do children assess each other's work?

Is there a whole-school policy on assessment?

Is your planning, recording and assessment linked?

The term ended with four members of the ATW being seconded from their schools for the Autumn term in order to deliver the National Curriculum Key Stage 1 training for all Infant, Special and Primary schools. This was to amount to 48 training days in that term, and the long process of planning began in the Summer term. This was just part of the overall plan indicated below, and it must be said that the actual days reflected very little of the initial tentative suggestions for their content. Meetings held with the ATW inspectors and advisory teachers eventually resulted in a day which was reassuring and generally helpful to colleagues, this being stated in the majority of evaluations. Once more we felt that it was only as a result of many minds coming together that the programme began to match needs. An undoubted strength of the day was that ATW who were delivering it were themselves practising teachers. Our training continues, as does future planning and preparation, and everyone involved continues to learn and grow.

Figure 8.4: Continuing Training Programme

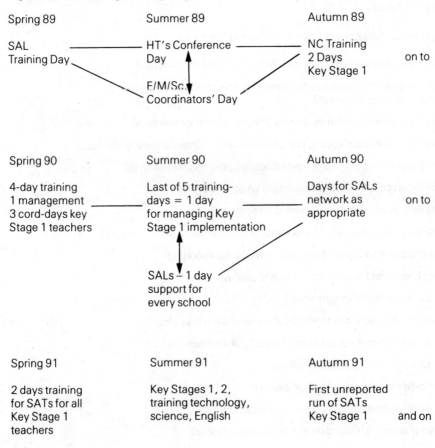

Spring 89	Summer 89	Autumn 89
SAL Training Day	HT's Conference Day	NC Training 2 Days Key Stage 1 — on to
	F/M/Sc. Coordinators' Day	

Spring 90	Summer 90	Autumn 90
4-day training 1 management 3 cord-days key Stage 1 teachers	Last of 5 training-days = 1 day for managing Key Stage 1 implementation	Days for SALs network as appropriate — on to
	SALs – 1 day support for every school	

Spring 91	Summer 91	Autumn 91
2 days training for SATs for all Key Stage 1 teachers	Key Stages 1, 2, training technology, science, English	First unreported run of SATs Key Stage 1 — and on

That it was written by teachers was a strength of the resource folder, which arrived in our schools towards the end of the Summer term. A questionnaire, which gave us an unexpectedly high response, revealed that many schools had used the folder and had found it helpful. Areas of concern and need were identified. It had been a disappointment to the team that the folder had not been produced by the end of April as originally hoped, but it was a mammoth task and the delay surprised few — we were grateful that it was at last in schools! A new ATW was formed in July, including eight members of the original team. This team was to review and revise the folder to try to meet the needs of the SALs. This second phase has been continuing during this academic year. The team feels that the folder offers no simple answers — there are none; but we hope that it may provide a vehicle for working together in developing policy. It is not seen as definitive, even in its revised state, but rather as a means of promoting discussion and thought, and, we hope, eventually, a whole-school approach towards making assessment a process which is first and foremost intended to support the children in Essex schools, as well as their teachers, in this period of considerable change.

Case Study 2

Planning Assessment and Recording a Whole-school Approach (Stephen Benyon)

Details of School

The school was built in the mid-1860s to serve its local village and outlying hamlets. The Victorian building was extended in the late 70s to accommodate children from the local army barracks. At present there are approximately 100 children on roll with an even split between military and civilian families. The school is Church-controlled and has close links with the village community, local farmers, the Anglican Church and a Non-conformist Church.

The school is staffed with a head teacher plus three full-time teachers, and a part-time teacher to assist with the head's class. The school also has a full-time clerical assistant and two part-time non-teaching assistants. Between them the staff are able to provide curriculum leadership in all the core subjects as well as expertise in the areas of information technology, music and drama. The staff are relatively young yet providing a broad range of experience.

The philosophy of the school is based upon a child-centred approach encouraging the children to work together in a harmonious and friendly atmosphere. The curriculum is organized upon a broad range of subjects with the learning situations being designed appropriately for each individual. Work is organized through a topic approach and arises from first-hand experience. The children are encouraged to record their responses in a variety of ways.

INSET and staff-development programmes have traditionally been organized on an informal basis. Unfortunately, this led to little written material being produced and needed attention. During the previous two years the school had been a leading force in organizing a local support cluster group for schools of a similar size. This work enabled us to look outside our own situation and learn from the experience of others in similar circumstances.

Aims and Proposed Timetable

The aim was to evolve a planning assessment and recording policy which would encompass the requirements of the National Curriculum without losing the particular features of the present practice in the school.

Particular concerns were that the demands of the National Curriculum should not distort or skew the work presently based on children's needs, interests and first-hand experiences. The timetable for thinking about these issues was as follows:

November 1988 — pre-planning.

January 1989 — INSET input to cluster group by Education Psychology Service on 'School strategies to develop learning strengths'.

January 1989 — joint planning for whole-school topic through which we could review assessment and recording strategies, progression and continuity, and identify ways of collecting samples of children's work that would be meaningful and purposeful.

April 1989 — review progress and prepare draft policy.

September 1989 — implement policy.

Starting Points

At the beginning of this work we were careful to bear in mind the comments made in paragraph 2 of the Report of the Task Group on Assessment and Testing which identified the following for any school to function effectively:

146

clear aims and objectives;
ways of gauging the achievement of these;
comprehensible language for communicating . . . achievements.

We began with a series of staff meetings during the Autumn term 1988. The focus of these meetings was initially assessment within the then existing curriculum framework. At this point the statutory orders for the core subjects were not available, but the reports of the science and mathematics working groups gave us an indication of the likely legal requirements.

The first meeting centred around an assessment review in which we considered the following questions:

where are we now?
are we assessing?
what do we assess?
what type of assessment takes place?
what strategies do we adopt?
do we record this information?
how can we refine/improve our practice?

We found this discussion reassuring in that we were able to recognize that our present assessment procedures were part of our normal classroom practice, and that, with a few exceptions, we had many of the skills required even if some needed further practise. We did discover, however, that our strategies were very diverse and not always appropriate to the task in hand. Recording our assessment was an area that needed major attention.

The second meeting concentrated, firstly, on identifying the ideal scenario and then considering how we might apply this to our own situation. We agreed to consider using a whole-school topic in the Spring term 1989 as a vehicle to try various ideas in planning, assessment and recording. These ideas were seen as a developmental process which would inform further discussions during the Summer term 1989 which would then help us formulate a policy.

The third meeting took our agreed ideas from the second meeting as a starting point, as well as the suggestion that we looked more closely at skills, attitudes, explorations, investigations, experiences and communication when planning our learning opportunities.

Planning

We realized that we would need to take account of the National Curriculum programmes of Study in our planning, but final versions of these were not available, and only draft versions available in mathematics and science. We therefore found the HMI 'Curriculum Matters' series very useful in giving us a guide to broad outlines in the other curriculum areas. One advantage of this approach was that through preparing our own schemes of work we began to identify aims and learning objectives which were to prove clearer and more meaningful than the eventual attainment targets included in the National Curriculum statutory orders.

Traditionally, each teacher had planned to use a 'topic web' which provided a flexible structure to the proposed experiences and learning opportunities. In addition to this web, staff gave learning-objective outlines in each of the curriculum areas. These plans were shared with colleagues at the beginning of each term when we were all able to contribute and make positive suggestions. Final versions of the plan were copied and given to the headteacher. This process enabled all staff to be fully informed of work being undertaken throughout the school, and, indeed, encouraged the children to show an active interest in the work being pursued by other children because we as a staff could draw on other children's work in a more informed way. This practice reinforced the school approach to the sharing of information and resources.

We looked at a variety of planning formats with a view to adopting a standard approach. However, we eventually agreed that whilst there would be common features in our planning, teachers would continue to present their plans in an individual way. Areas to be addressed included balance within a topic and over the whole year, use of resources (including other adults), use of the local environment, display, and children's participation in the process.

Assessment

In developing our approaches to assessment we bore in mind the four purposes outlined in the TGAT report and in Chapter 2, and identified those that we would need to be particularly concerned with in the immediate future. These were diagnostic and formative assessment.

In considering our approach to diagnostic assessment, we were able to build on our recent review of provision for children with special educational needs, which had been a major focus of our school and cluster INSET during 1987–8. Our special-needs support teacher provided examples of diagnostic assessment which enabled us to clarify our thinking.

Formative assessment was seen to be a natural part of the learning process and not an extra activity during the school week. We agreed to trial a variety of approaches and drew heavily upon the strategies section of the Essex Assessment Initiative Children's Assessment Pack. We were careful to match assessment strategies to the activities in which the children were engaged. We were particularly concerned to involve the children in the process and to give them responsibility to engage in self-asssessment.

One consequence of our trials was careful consideration of classroom organization and the storing of equipment. We already had a policy of encouraging children to be independent, and this was further encouraged. Teachers made a conscious effort to spend more time in discussion with pupils, allowing children to express their responses rather than assuming them from a distance. Time was found for observations which contributed greatly to our knowledge of how children approached certain tasks and interacted with other children.

Strategies tried included tape recording, conferencing, teachers and children keeping diaries, field notes, video and photographs.

The photographs provided an excellent means through which the children could recall feelings of success and frustration, and of recording models and joint efforts at display. They also provided a visual stimulus for younger children to talk through chronologically an experiment of investigation.

The use of a video-camera provided valuable INSET material for all the staff which contributed greatly to our concerns regarding progression and continuity. The children's response was also valuable in making them more aware of their strategies to investigations.

Throughout this process, the staff found that the assessments were contributing to future planning both in the short term and the long term. Indeed, one teacher used the weekly planning sheet as a way of recording 'on the spot' assessments.

Recording

The school had existing records for language development, reading and mathematics. These needed to be amended to accommodate the requirements of the National Curriculum, but we did feel that to record only progress through the statements of attainment was inadequate. We were also concerned that the children should have some ownership of the process, as well as ensuring that not all recording should be in a written format.

Staff encouraged the children to contribute to the recording of their activities and achievements, and this in turn provided the children with evidence upon which to base their own assessments. The children's involvement in this way allowed the teacher to concentrate on the children's responses to activities and experiences rather than just noting that work was completed.

The involvement of the children also provided the teachers with information which enabled them to reflect upon curriculum provision and identify whether specific needs were being met.

Teachers' records included diaries with pages for individual children, whilst others were in the form of identified targets written in the form of 'can do' statements. Another format was a list of skills, attitudes, etc., some common to all pupils whilst others were particular. These entries were highlighted in a colour-coded system to indicate level of response.

Review

At the end of the Spring term 1989 we collected together all the various materials and ideas that staff had trialled. This enabled us to prepare a draft policy statement for planning assessment and recording (the statement is provided as an appendix).

The draft policy then became a working document for future reference during the Summer term 1989 and also Autumn term 1989. During these terms more information became available with regard to legal requirements, and so the policy could be adapted as appropriate. A final version could then be prepared during the Summer term 1990 (note a change of time-scale from the original plan) when the regulations for assessment and reporting would be available. The draft regulations on reporting were published in January 1990, and a final version is expected in July 1990. The draft assessment regulations are expected during April 1990, with a final version being published during the Autumn 1990.

We also became aware that our existing school curriculum policy documents were inadequate in that they only provided a broad outline and did not indicate a clear scheme of work or specific aims and learning objectives. We therefore decided to begin a process of updating and rewriting these policies within a new timetable.

June 1989 — revision of school general aims
Autumn term 1990 — rewriting of mathematics policy
by December 1989 — produce science policy
Spring term 1989 — rewriting of English policy
April 1990 — review draft policy on planning, assessment and recording
Summer term 1990 — the development of an 'umbrella policy' for a topic-work approach in the National Curriculum, which will stress the unique characteristics of our school curriculum, based upon the local environment and use of local resources.

Summer term 1990 — review record-keeping in light of changes to policy documents and regulations.

Update

In producing a mathematics policy, the format for a scheme of work evolved into a formative record as well (this is provided as an appendix). Narrative comment is needed for attainment targets 1 and 9 which are seen as the key to effective learning in mathematics. A similar model is being adapted for science, with attainment target 1 being of paramount importance.

In seeking to draw all the elements of planning, assessment and recording into a cohesive whole, the school is to adopt a primary version of records of achievement which will include:

the children recording their achievements both in and out of school;

involving the children in the assessment, recording and reporting process;

widening the review process to include parents;

indicating to the children that they have a major role to play in reflecting on their responses;

building up a child's selection of work that is representative of a broad and balanced curriculum.

The school has now developed the following model for continuous review of the curriculum through the assessment process.

Figure 8.5 Planning, Assessment and Recording Model

A DRAFT POLICY STATEMENT — This is a developing policy which will be finalized during the Summer term 1990 when further information is available.

PLANNING

The importance of planning cannot be underestimated in the light of the requirements of the National Curriculum and also in response to the need to provide a quality education for all pupils which is based upon a broad, balanced, relevant and differentiated curriculum.

Planning, in whatever form of presentation, must take account of the following:

the school's general aims;
the requirement to teach National Curriculum Programmes of Study;
cross-curricular issues;
religious education;
appropriate and relevant starting points;
continuity and progression in skills development;
classroom organization and use of resources;
classroom display.

It is intended to move from termly planning to yearly planning and eventually a two-year plan based upon the development of children's skills, attitudes and experiences rather than pre-determined content.

Detailed plans will need to be completed termly and updated half-termly with copies held by the headteacher.

The present practice of shared planning will continue, but will need to become more forward looking.

Plans should clearly indicate objectives for each area of learning experience, and identify the possible activities in which children may engage.

Staff may need to maintain more detailed personal plans which will cover activities and particular targets for individuals or groups of children.

Where appropriate, daily plans may be designed in line with the school's Special Needs Policy.

ASSESSMENT

The assessment of children's progress should be a natural part of the learning process. The children should be clear about what is expected of them and have some understanding of what is necessary to achieve success.

The children should play an active part in the assessment process.

The positive aspects should always be stressed, and when reviewing progress with the children, what can be done should be emphasized rather than what cannot be done.

The use of formative and diagnostic assessment should inform the planning process and the setting of appropriate targets for all children.

A variety of methods of assessment can be adopted, as indicated in the strategy section of the Essex Assessment Initiative pack. Selected strategies should be appropriate to the task/activity upon which the children are engaged.

Teachers should take care to record the purpose of assessment, strategy adopted and the outcome. This process will inform future planning.

At all times, staff should seek to be as objective as possible and be particularly aware of cultural bias and preconceived notions.

Presently summative assessment occurs through the use of the following County prescribed tests:

Young's Group Reading Test (Spring term, year-2 children)
NFER Reading Comprehension DE (Spring term, year-6 children)

NFER Essex mathematics 1A and 1B tests (Spring term, year-6 children)

Evaluative assessment will occur as part of the process of regular school reviews under the auspices of the County Inspectorate.

RECORD-KEEPING

Records have traditionally served a variety of purposes and audiences. Our aim is to develop a cohesive approach to record-keeping which will inform all entitled persons.

Teachers' personal records will continue to play an important role in aiding memory and forming assessments.

Records will reflect the school's aims and objectives, and be drawn from detailed curriculum schemes of work.

Samples of children's work will be kept as records, not only of the product, but as an indication of the process. Children's work should be annotated with relevant details such as date, context and what achievements the work represents.

Opportunities will be provided for children to keep records of their own tasks, including review of their own response to their activities. This will lead in time to the development of self-assessment by all children.

Records will need to be accessible to children, parents and teachers, along with appropriate planning information.

May 1989.

Figure 8.6: Curriculum Plan – Mathematics

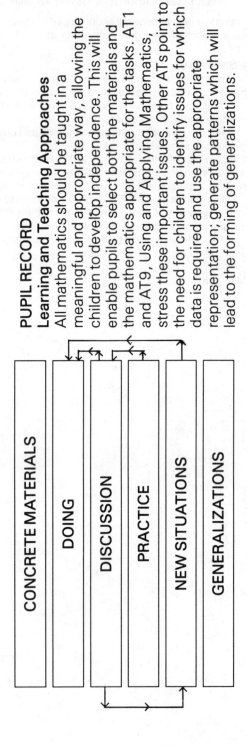

DEBDEN C.E. PRIMARY SCHOOL

Mathematics

CURRICULUM PLAN

(incorporating Scheme of Work and
Programmes of Study Key Stages 1 and 2)

PUPIL RECORD
Learning and Teaching Approaches

All mathematics should be taught in a
meaningful and appropriate way, allowing the
children to develop independence. This will
enable pupils to select both the materials and
the mathematics appropriate for the tasks. AT1
and AT9, Using and Applying Mathematics,
stress these important issues. Other ATs point to
the need for children to identify issues for which
data is required and use the appropriate
representation; generate patterns which will
lead to the forming of generalizations.

CONCRETE MATERIALS

DOING

DISCUSSION

PRACTICE

NEW SITUATIONS

GENERALIZATIONS

AT 1/9 L1	AT 1/9 L2	AT 1/9 L3	AT 1/9 L4	AT5 L4	AT 1/9 L5	AT 1/9 L6	AT5 L6b	AT8 L6b	AT12 L6
use materials for a practical task. talk about own work and ask questions. make predictions based upon experience.	select materials and mathematics to use for a practical task. describe work and check results. ask and respond to the question 'what would happen if...?'.	select the materials and mathematics for a task. check results, consider if they are sensible. explain work and record findings in a systematic way. make and test predictions.	select the materials and mathematics for a task. plan work methodically. record findings, present them in visual, oral or written form. use examples to test statements or definitions.	apply strategies to explore number patterns and properties. generalize, mainly in words, patterns which arise in various situations.	select the materials and mathematics for a task: check there is sufficient information: work methodically, review progress. interpret mathematical information presented in visual, oral or written form. make and test simple statements.	design a task, select the mathematics and resources; check information and obtain what is missing; use 'trial and improve' methods. present findings using visual, oral or written forms. make and test general statements and simple hypotheses; define and reason with some precision.	use spreadsheets to explore number sequences.	recognize that measurement is approximate; choose the degree of accuracy appropriate for the situation.	identify issues for which data is required: design. use appropriate observation sheet to collect data: collate, analyse results. design a questionnaire to survey opinion: collate, analyse results.

Early Years

Possible Experiences	Possible Knowledge	Sets	Shape	Capacity	Handling Data
sorting and matching through tactile and visual experiences. 3-D modelling e.g. clay. building and constructing e.g. large and small bricks. fitting together and pulling apart e.g. large jigsaws or mechanical toys. free play: sand, water. pouring; liquids, grains, seeds.	sort and match objects with common feature. basic colours. identify body parts. familiar with some number rhymes. make patterns with beads, bricks etc. know that clocks tell time. know that money is used in shopping. use words to describe direction, speed, position. describe similar and different things.	sort by 1 attribute. 2 attributes represent sets in a physical way e.g. group of children or objects. **Number** know that last count in set is total of set. 2.1/b conservation of number. count 1–4 1–5 6–10 10–20 2.1/a order 1–4 1–5 6–10 10–20 read 1–4 0–5 6–10 2.1/a write 1–4 0–5 6–10 **Money** 2.1/a read value on 1p, 2p, 5p, 10p coins. know that size does not represent value of coin. simple shopping.	paint faces on 3-D shapes. free play with 3-D shapes, 2-D shapes. 10,1/b sort 2-D shapes, 3-D shapes. use 10,1/a 2-D shapes to make patterns and pictures. 10,1/b use interlocking shapes puzzles and 'feely box'. **Area** painting to cover surfaces. use paper, shapes etc. to cover surfaces. **Space** use common prepositions to describe position in relation to own body. other objects. know left and right on own body.	sand play. water play. understand full and empty. idea of half full and half empty. **Length** understand long, short. use own body as a measure. **Weight** use a balance. understand heavy, light. **Time** recognize terms: day night morning afternoon lunchtime etc. daily events: weekly events yearly events.	13.1/a use of 3-D objects to represent data. **Maths Games** use of board games and 'snakes and ladder' type games. use of dice and counters. use of number cards.

Key Stage One

Language

Ref	Content
	use as appropriate estimate, guess, more less, fewer, greater, long, short, tall, small, thick, thin, fat, narrow, heavy, light, hot, cold (and -er -est forms) difference add, plus, subtract, minus, lots of, share, coin, change, value, before, after, colours, deep, pale, rough, smooth
2,2a	

Sets

Ref	Content
12,1	able to sort objects, people, attribute blocks with given criteria, own selected criteria.
13,1b	recognize subsets, empty sets, union and inter-section. mapping of sets, attribute block games.
5,1	predicting patterns using beads, bricks, attribute blocks, etc.

Number

Ref	Content
2,2a	recognize, count and order 0-10, 11-20, 21-99, 100 write (numerals) 0-10, 11-20, 21-100 write (words) 1-10
5,3c	count back 10, 9, 8, etc. count on in 2s, 3s, 5s, 10s. skip count from any number.
4,1	estimate to 10; to 20
4,2	number bonds to 5, to 10.
5,2a	mapping addition to 10, subtraction from 10.
3,1	differences between single-digit numbers.
3,2b	addition and subtraction. - 10
3,2a	- 20
3,3a	repeated addition.
5,2b	subtraction. number sequences. odd and even.
	recognize symbols + - x ÷ = < > ordinal numbers to 10.

Money

Ref	Content
	sort and match coins.
3,2c	recognize and use 1p, 2p, 5p, 10p, 20p, 50p, £1.
8,2b	shopping to 5p, 10p, 20p, 50p, £1. shopping including change. equivalence of coins.

Math Games

Ref	Content
14,1	make predictions regarding possible outcomes.
14,2	design games and invent new rules for existing ones.

Measures

Ref	Content
8,1	comparison in length, weight, capacity. conservation of length, weight, capacity.
8,1	ordering length, weight, capacity. use of abitrary measures, length (inc own body measures)
8,2a	weight, capacity. recognize and use litres (1/2), pints (1/2), kg (1/2, 1/4), g (500, 200, 100), km (1/2, 1/4), m (1/2, 1/4), mile.
8,2c	

Time

Ref	Content
	succession of events: yesterday, today, tomorrow. days of the week. birthdays. months of the year. use of arbitrary units,
8,2a	
8,2c	recognize and use hour. read digital time. 1/2, 1/4 hour. experiences in intervals of seconds, minutes.
8,3c	

Space

Ref	Content
11,1a	use and follow appropriate language for direction, position.
11,1b	
10,2b	identify right angles in 2-D and 3-D shapes and in everyday objects. use own body to turn 90°, left, right,
11,2a	
11,3b	clockwise, and anti-clockwise and describe this. give instructions to others to turn.
11,2b	use 4 point compass. appreciate movement along a line. translation, rotation, reflection.

Area

Ref	Content
11,2c	comparison of everyday objects ordering of 2-D shapes. use of arbitrary units to measure area. use of □ paper as standard unit.

Shape

Ref	Content
10,2a	identify cube, cuboid, sphere. cylinder as shapes and as everyday objects. identify circles, rectangles, squares, pentagons, hexagons as shapes and as faces of 3-D shapes. use appropriate language to describe 2-D and 3-D shapes.
10,3	tessellate 2-D shapes to form new shapes.

Handling Data

Ref	Content
	use of symbols to represent real objects/people etc. sort and classify data recording in tally charts, Venn diagrams, frequency tables, block graphs, Carroll diagrams. read and interpret the above. use of 'Datapack' or similar to store and retrieve data.
12,2a	
12,2b	
13,2a	
13,2b	
12,3a	
12,3b	

Key Stage Two (i)

Number/Algebra

Code	Content
2,3a	recognize, use, order nos. to 500, 1000, beyond 1000.
2,4a	count forward, back in 10s, 100s, 1000s from any point.
3,4b	2-digit nos. × 1-digit nos. 2-digit nos. + 1-digit nos. problems using everyday above. + – using tenths, hundredths.
3,4c	recognize, use number, patterns.
5,3a	predict sequence.
3,4c	recognize, use common fractions 1/2, 1/3, 1/4, 1/5, 1/10, 1/100.
2,3a	place value, understand relationships between
2,4f	recognize, use common % 100%, 50%, 25%, 10%. × places, effect of × 10, × 100.
2,4e	× as inverse of ÷.
6,4b	use LOGO to show forward as inverse of back.
3,3c	multiplication division, facts to 10 × 10.
3,4a	digital root patterns. associative law: 3 × (2 × 4) = (3 × 2) × 4, commutative law: 3 × 7 = 7 × 3, use
3,4b	mentally + – 2-digit nos. + several 1-digit nos. + – to 999. negative whole nos. e.g. temperature scale.
2,3c	approximate to nearest 10, 100. negatives on calculator.
4,3a	remainders, 'rounding off' estimate
4,3b	answers. use calculator to check validity.
4,4a	Roman numerals, other number systems. input, output
6,3	functions.

Length

Code	Content
8,3c	estimates, use trundle wheels, tapes etc.
8,3b	introduce cm and mm with relationship between km, m, cm, mm.
8,3a / 8,4a / 8,5c	calculations
2,4c	using cm as 1/100m and 0.01m.

Capacity and Volume

Code	Content
8,3c	estimates, meaning of capacity (space in) and volume (space filled).
8,3a / 8,4a / 8,5c	conservation of volume. count cubes for volume. introduce ml and relationship to l. calibrate own measures.

Weight

Code	Content
8,3b	use scales for personal weights.
8,3a	relationship between g and kg. estimates.
8,4a	
8,5c	problems using + – × ÷.

Time

Code	Content
8,3b	Investigate water clocks, egg timers, pendulum, sundials, links between digital and analogue clocks. reading minutes to and past.
8,4a	relationship between seconds, minutes, hours, day. 24hr clock. estimation. timetables.

Money

Code	Content
2,3b	equivalence to 50p, £1. shopping to £1. shopping to £10. decimal notation 1p = 1/100£ = £0.01 + – × + problems reflecting everyday situations.
3,3b	

Sets

Code	Content
6,3	universal set, subsets. matrix games using attribute blocks. classify numbers into sets of primes, square, triangular etc. relationship (function) between sets of numbers.
6,4a	identify operators in mappings between sets.

Space

Code	Content
11,3b	8 point compass. use coordinates to specify location in 1st quadrant.
7,4	develop idea of angle, distance to specify location.
10,4a	
11,4a	

Shape

Code	Content
10,4b	investigate edges, faces, vertices. explore nets. build 3-D shapes.
11,3a	investigate reflective symmetry, rotational symmetry.
11,4b	explore properties of 2-D shapes. arrange into sets and subsets. widen range of known shapes e.g. rhombus etc. use
10,4b	geoboard to create shapes. notion of perimeter. tessellate using regular and irregular shapes. make right angles by folding.

Area

Code	Content
8,4b	investigate relationship between shape and area e.g. △ and □s to count □s to determine area of regular and irregular shapes. introduce standard units cm²/sq.cm.

Probability

Code	Content
14,3b	introduce permutations and Cartesian products. idea of evens. order events according to
14,3a	'likelihood'. idea of 'fair' test. devise
14,3c	number games.

Handling Data

Code	Content
13,3b	create and interpret pictograms. construct and interpret bar-line graphs, line graphs and frequency diagrams.
13,4b	create and use decision tree diagrams.
13,4c	
13,4d	identify issues for which data collection is appropriate e.g. personal data, weather statistics. use class intervals when appropriate.
13,4a	
12,4a	use a database to interrogate data. idea of average, mean and range of data.
13,5c	
12,4c	
12,4b	

Key Stage Two (ii)

Number	Algebra	Measures	Time	Space/Shape	Probability
recognize and use large nos. understand relationship between place values: ×10, ÷10, ×100, ÷100, ×1000, ÷1000. 3-digit nos. × 2-digit nos. 3-digit nos. ÷ 2-digit nos. — 3.5a nos. place value to 3rd dec. pl. + − × ÷ involving decimals, using money and measures. budgeting e.g. school events etc. — 2.6a approximate calculations, rounding to sig. fig. or dec. pl. interpreting calculator displays, e.g. 6.333333, calculate %s using calculator where appropriate. fractions of whole nos. equivalence of fractions, decimals, %s. use negative nos. in context. estimation in calculations. — 4.5b, 4.4b, 4.4c, 3.5b, 3.6a, 2.6b, 3.6c, 3.5d, 4.5a, 4.6	number patterns: Sieve of Eratosthenes — 5.5c Fibonacci Sequence. Pascal's Triangle. — 5.6a relationship between □ nos, △ nos, etc. factors, multiples. idea of indices. □ root, ⊕ root. — 5.5b ratio, direct proportion. — 3.5c, 2.5a, 5.5a scale. LOGO commands in plot points, in 1st quadrant, in 4 quadrants. define shapes. — 3.6b, 2.5b, 2.6b use map references, bearings. — 7.5, 10.6c, 11.6d understand. use simple formula — 11.6a expressed in words or symbols. — 6.5a, 6.5b	conversion of metric to common Imperial equivalents. — 8.5b use of spring balance. calibration of own spring. recording length, weight, capacity to 3 dec. pl. 1 litre as 1000cm³. measuring volume by displacement 1 litre water weighs 1kg. idea of mass, density. reading distances on maps. — 8.5a **Area** estimates, explore relationship of area to perimeter. relationship of area of □ to △ with same base. plans drawn to scale. area of circle and irregular shapes using a variety of practical approaches. relationship between cm² and m². — 8.4c, 8.5a	use of timers, record time to 1/10, 1/100 second. speed, time, distance. — 8.6a notion of average speed. history of calendar. time in relation to Earth's movement. **Handling Data** use of graph paper. defining of axes. use of scale. collect, order, record continuous data. create data files and interrogate files. handle, record data collected from experiments. construct, read, interpret pie charts conversion graphs. plot time, speed, distance graphs, read and interpret. create, use scatter graphs, matrices, networks. — 12.5a, 12.5c, 12.5b, 13.5a, 13.5b, 13.6a, 13.6b, 13.6c	understand, use language associated with angles. explain, use angle — 10.5b properties. recognize, use symmetrical properties of 2-D & 3-D shapes. use isometric paper to represent 3-D shapes in 2-D. classify 2-D shapes by properties. plot points to draw lines, figures in 1st quadrant, in 4 quadrants. use clinometer, protractor, compass, set square etc. construction of 2-D shapes. congruence of simple shapes. use a mirror line to reflect shapes. enlarge shapes by whole number scale factors. use networks to solve problems. — 10.6a, 11.5a, 10.6b, 10.6d, 11.5c, 8.5d, 10.5a, 11.6b, 11.6c, 11.5b	recognize, use probability scale 0-1, estimate possible outcomes. list all possible outcomes. aware that different outcomes may occur from the same event. distinguish between estimates based upon symmetry and those based on statistics. understand that if a range of events is equally likely (n) then the probability of one occurring is 1/n. identify all outcomes from 2 combined events which are independent. k that the total of all possible outcomes is 1 and the probability of an outcome is 1 minus the probability of it not happening. — 14.4a, 14.4b, 14.4c, 14.5a, 14.5b, 14.5c, 14.6a, 14.6b

Chapter 9

Conclusion

A central theme of this book has been that interpreting assessment as a research-based activity not only provides evidence to satisfy National Curriculum requirements, but also informs us of the success of our teaching and improves our understanding of the nature of the learning process. By implication, the act of assessment is part and parcel of a school's evaluation. As long ago as 1969, Robert Schaeffer argued that schools should become *centres of inquiry*, which, he suggested, should occur at five levels:

They should allow teachers to undertake systematic investigations of their own practice in their own classrooms.

Wherever possible, these investigations should be seen as collaborative enterprises, not only between colleagues in school but via links with higher education.

The pupils/students should be encouraged to become active learners, engaged in their own assessment of their progress in order for them to become continuous, reflective learners.

The school should work towards becoming 'a learning organization', that is, one that provides a supportive context for learning at all levels, of adults and children alike.

In-service opportunities should be meaningful experiences providing the participants with a 'trained capacity for inquiry and assessment'.

The ideas advocated by Schaeffer have been adapted recently by Holly (1989a), who suggests that the information collected for assessment purposes also offers useful information that could be used in developmental appraisal, for internal evaluation and accountability and for external evaluation and accountability. He argues that it would be most productive for a school to create a means of organizing and processing the information collected from assessment, evaluation and appraisal, which could then be used for a variety of purposes.

> Moreover all those concerned with the school...can see themselves as both creators of data...and users of this same data...The data can be used for:
>
> > teacher reflection/action research and team-based collaborative inquiry;
> >
> > student assessment, including progress, guidance and negotiated learning;
> >
> > reporting (and talking) to parents and the community within what can be a two-way dialogue of listening and informing;
> >
> > the profiling of school-based development. (Holly, 1989b)

As we have seen for pupils, profiling allows for a greater range of achievement to be recognized. This could also be the same for a school, if it were possible to create a research-based register of the full range of achievements and successes of a school — all supported by evidence of the kind advocated by Holly. As Deal has commented:

> Excellence or improvement cannot be installed or mandated from outside; it must be developed from within. It must arise from collective conversations, behaviours and spirit among teachers, administrators, students and parents within a local school community. (Deal, 1984)

In 1986, the Carnegie Report into the state of Education in the United States argued that the focus of schools needed to shift from teaching to learning, from the passive acquisition of facts to the active application of ideas to problems. Teachers were fundamental in this process, but to be successful:

> Teachers must think for themselves if they are to help others think for themselves, be able to act independently and collaborate with others, and render critical judgement...[what are required are] schools in which authority is grounded in the professional competence of the teacher, and where teachers work together as colleagues, constantly striving to improve their performance. (Carnegie Report, 1986)

Derek Rowntree concluded his book on assessment with a variety of pertinent points, many of which still stand the test of time. Amongst his comments he suggested that:

> We should make as clear as possible the criteria by which we assess. This is of benefit to us as well as the children. 'Let us strive to become more aware of our implicit assessment constructs and constantly question why we value the qualities we do.' This has to

be undertaken as a whole-school activity as well as by individual teachers in their own classrooms.

Attempt to be adventurous in our choice of assessment methods, recognizing that different methods elicit different qualities. We need to develop our skills of selecting the most effective method to draw out the qualities being sought.

As Black *et al.* (1989) suggested, 'Since the primary school has long prided itself on the variety of experiences it offers to children in a carefully-balanced curriculum, assessment should reflect this balance'.

Primary schools have prided themselves on the space they offer for opportunistic learning, taking advantage of the unintended. We need to allow for this in our assessments. Give credit for what has been learned, not just what it was intended should have been learned.

Wherever possible 'naturalistic' assessment procedures, which concentrate on process and products pursued for their own educational sakes are more appropriate — rather than devising exercises solely for assessment purposes which may not be quality learning experiences.

Always provide maximum feedback to children about their assessments, by relating subsequent teaching to those assessments, or by making clear which qualities have been discerned and achieved and where effort is still needed.

Where assessments are evaluative rather than descriptive we should make clear the standard against which the work is being compared.

We should learn to accept that equally perceptive colleagues might hold quite different opinions. We need to learn to take comment from others as information rather than personal critique. If there is a difference of opinion, it should lead us to search for other information to confirm or check judgements rather than react emotionally.

Resist the temptation to concentrate on qualities, skills and knowledge that are easy to measure and less likely to provoke disagreement. It is through the constructive use of difference that we can learn and thus extend our thinking.

We need to encourage children to become participants in their own assessment — the development of the reflective learner as well as the reflective teacher.

Some time ago I came across a lovely story in the *Times Educational Supplement* by Jacqui Travens. It was called 'In the altogether' and concerned the loss of salary-negotiating rights of teachers and the extensive demands being placed upon them by society. I have adapted this story to conclude this book, so, with apologies to Jacqui Travens:

> Once upon a time in 1990 in the Land of Primary Education, the rulers decreed that all who answered *I will*, would be praised indeed.
>
> They asked,
>
> Will you educate children to cope with Birth, Life and Death,
>
> Help them to explore the Environment near and far;
>
> Teach about our heritage;
>
> Educate for today's multi-cultured society?
>
> And for the future,
>
> Prevent football hooliganism and all anti-social behaviour,
>
> Teach pupils their own and other Religions,
>
> Teach all aspects of the National Curriculum, allocating each sufficient time for it to be experienced in depth?
>
> Will you also ensure that achievement is properly assessed so that it is fair to the children, revealing to the teacher and informative to the parents?
>
> And we each answered — *I will*!
>
> They asked,
>
> Will you cover your walls with children's original work, triple-mounted, but without wasting materials?
>
> Change displays frequently,
>
> Allow hours, even weeks for one piece of work to achieve perfection?
>
> Will you make each day child-centred, different, exciting, challenging, yet have pupils so familiar with a routine that they can work independently?
>
> Again, we answered — I will!
>
> Will you remember to produce appropriate tokens for Easter, Mother's Day, Christmas and all other festivals,
>
> Provide entertainment for parents,
>
> Attend evening and holiday in-service sessions,
>
> Collect book boxes from county library,
>
> Re-useable cardboard from Sainsbury's,
>
> Off-cuts from local factories,
>
> Devise money-making schemes for the school to support Local Management and paint the classrooms?
>
> To which we answered – I will.
>
> And I add at the end of this:
>
> > and, dear Lord, when they have achieved all of this, move over.

Appendix A

Structuring Observations

Kathy Sylva, Marjorie Painter, Carolyn Roy

Why Observe?

Watching is commonplace behaviour; we do it surreptitiously when in public, more openly when we believe that we, the obsevers, are not ourselves observed. There are countless motives for watching others. First, there is ordinary curiosity. But we also watch to gain information useful in achieving specific goals. One such goal might be the creation of rich environments for children, and there follow suggestions for observing them in their preschool habitat.

The 'target child' method of observing has been stolen — in a respectable, scientific way — from people who study animal behaviour. Curious as to the ways animals adapt to both the physical and social environment, ethologists donned sturdy field-gear and followed individual animals around woodland, plain and desert. They recorded minute aspects of behaviour, making notes on social interaction, feeding habits, cooperative and defensive activity. They learned the peculiar habits of individual animals, but equally valuable were the pictures they pieced together of how animals in various categories (e.g. young infants, mothers, or male juveniles) behaved in everyday situations.

Formal observation of animals and preschool children is a far cry from casual watching. To begin, the observer makes notes and pores over them after observation. Field notes are then coded and quantified. No one, even the most innocent, watches with a completely open mind. We select certain bits of activity as 'interesting' or 'important' and exclude the rest. We are often unaware of the process of selecting and interpreting, but it is always with us. The 'target child' technique makes explicit its ways of filtering and interpreting. You may query its methods, or even change them, but it will make you confront the preconceptions that you bring with you to the task.

How to Observe?

Decide *which child* to observe. You may have a reason for choosing a particular child. Perhaps you simply don't know him well, or maybe his behaviour causes difficulty, or you suspect some abnormality. Otherwise it is a good idea to start by choosing a child at random. Pick a name randomly from the register, or choose, say, the first child you see wearing blue, or the first child to cross a particular spot on the floor or at a certain activity.

Before you start observing, make sure that *members of the staff* know what you are doing and that they understand that you will not intervene unless there is danger to children or property. This is particularly important if you work in the group where you are observing. Ask them to carry on normally, trying not to avoid the child you are watching nor spending an unusual amount of time with him.

When observing, try to become *'a fly on the wall'*, as inconspicuous as possible. If you can, get close enough to hear what the child says, but without his realizing that you are watching him. It is a good idea to sit or crouch sideways on to the child, not directly facing him. Try to avoid meeting his gaze. If he or another child speaks to you, of course answer him but as briefly and kindly as possible.

How long to observe? Aim at observing for 10 minutes. Later you may want to observe for longer, say 20 minutes, to get a fuller picture of what the child does.

Recording Your Observation

Use a ready drawn-up recording sheet as in Figure A1.1.

Have a watch, preferably with a second hand, so that you can record minute by minute. Observe for several minutes before you start to write anything down.

Write down *what the child does* in each minute in the *ACTIVITY* column. For instance, 'Pulls small lump off large piece of dough, squeezes it, watches child opposite'. Write down exactly what happens without adding any interpretation. Also jot down a note about the activity and materials and whether other children or adults are present. For example, 'Table with 2 large lumps of blue dough, 2 other children, helper sitting there'.

Write down what the child says and what other children or adults say to him, for each minute, in the *LANGUAGE* column. It is often impossible to write down the exact words spoken, but record the gist of comments if you can.

Figure A1.1 Blank Recording Sheet

CHILD'S INITIALS:	SEX:	AGE:	DATE AND TIME OBSERVED:		
ACTIVITY RECORD		LANGUAGE RECORD		TASK	SOCIAL
1					
2					
3					
4					
5					
6					
7					
8					
9					
10					

It is helpful to use the following abbreviations as a sort of short-hand to help you note down quickly what is done and said:

TC   Target child (the one you are observing)

C   Other child

A   Any adult (such as staff member, mother-helper, teenage student, the observer (you))

→   Speaks to

These abbreviations are especially useful in noting the language; here are some examples:

TC	Sings to self
TC→C	'I'm the father and you're the mother.'
C→TC	'You're not coming to my birthday party.'
A→TC	Comforts him
TC→A	'Will you tie my apron please?'
TC→C	Conversation
TC unison	Sings
A→Group	Announces milk-time
A→TC + C	Reads a story

Note: The LANGUAGE column does not include instances where the child is listening-in to another conversation without participating or being included. This would be written down in the ACTIVITY column.

If you are interrupted for a short time whilst observing, don't worry. Just note it as 'interruption'.

After your observation is finished, make a note of what the child does next. This may help you to make better sense of what he was doing at the end of the observation.

Looking for 'Themes'

When you have finished writing down your observation, go over it and divide it into separate spells of coherent activity; look for the themes in the child's activity. By a 'theme', we mean a continued stream of activity where the child is 'following a thread'.

Draw double lines across the page of your observation where one theme ends and another begins, so that you can readily see the start and end of each spell of activity.

The theme *may* be based on the materials which the child is using, or on the other children or adults that he's with. But sometimes the start and end of a theme do not coincide with what on the surface looks like a change in the type of activity itself.

Some examples:

(1) A child leaves the milk table and goes to the woodwork bench where he constructs an aeroplane, then he moves off to do a painting. From his movement towards the woodwork until his completing of the aeroplane and leaving the bench, is one theme. The painting begins a new theme — it is not connected with the woodwork.

But:
(2) A boy makes an aeroplane at the woodwork bench, then takes it to a table to paint it. Although he's using some different materials and changes from construction to painting, this is all one theme centred around the aeroplane.

(3) A child climbs up and slides down the slide, goes over to a large barrel and wriggles through it, then goes off to climb along a raised plank. All of this sequence involves body movement, but there are three separate themes.

But:
(4) A boy is with two friends playing 'follow-the-leader'. He follows his friends up and down the slide, through a barrel, along a plank. Here there is only one theme, with the different movements tied together by the flow of the follow-the-leader game.

Sometimes a child engages in a spell of sustained activity that has short interruptions in it. If an interruption lasts for only a minute, then ignore it when drawing the double lines for 'theme'.
An example:

A child spends several minutes painting, but stops for a minute to go over and talk to a friend before returning to her painting. Note this as all one theme, ignoring the brief chat.

Ignoring these small interruptions gives you a better idea of how long a child stays with an activity. Similarly, preparation for an activity (such as putting on an apron before water-play, fetching a helmet to pretend at being a fireman), or completing an activity (such as hanging up a painting), can be counted as part of the main theme.
The sample observation (Figure A1.2) may make this clearer.
Marking the start and end of the themes like this will give you an idea of how long a child sustains a theme in his play and how many themes may occur in an observation. You may then be able to see what it is that makes for long themes of play (interesting materials? other children? adult presence?)

Figure A1.2: Sample record

CHILD'S INITIALS: A.N. SEX: boy AGE: 4/11 DATE AND TIME OBSERVED: 18/11 10.50 am			
ACTIVITY RECORD	LANGUAGE RECORD	TASK	SOCIAL
1 TC at woodwork table, hammers nail into wood. Goes round table & looks at small metal pieces. Offers nail to A.	TC → A: Will you bang this? A → TC (bangs nail in)		
2 Watches A carefully. Gives A a bottle cap to hammer on for him	A → TC (about hammering) TC → A (asks her to hammer on cap)		
3 Watches A hammering his bottle cap & milk bottle top into wood with nail. A finishes – hands TC his wood. (looks like →			
4 Carries woodwork outside, back indoors. Takes it to paint. Paints it blue, with brush			
5 Paints his woodwork. Paints, wipes thumb on paper, on wood.			
6 Paints his woodwork.			
7 Takes coat off – gets apron and puts it on. Continues to paint	A → TC: Not with your coat on, you'll get it all over		
8 Paints woodwork	A → TC: Now finish that and come and have your milk. TC → A: No! A → TC: We'll save some then		
9 Looks at hands – goes to washbowl in corner (leaves woodwork on paint table) Washes with 1 C	TC ⟷ C TC ⟷ C A → TC + C (about washing)		
10 Washes hands, dries them. Goes to sit at milk table, next to twin brother. Helper gives him cup	TC → A: Wheres mine? I haven't got a cup. TC → C: I got a blue one		

and what brings themes of play to an end (completion? lack of ideas? distractions? interruptions?). You may want to see how often a child returns to a theme from a previous spell of play in one observation, or to see whether a child finds some themes more absorbing than others.

Coding Your Observation

Each minute's observation can be looked at in three different ways. They are:

The social code (whom the child is *with*)

This code analyses the observation in terms of the child's social interaction, or lack of it. For example, the *task code* tells us the child was, say, engaged in manipulative play, while the *social code* tells us he was chatting with a friend throughout it.

The language code (what the child *says* and what *is said* to him)

This code shows who spoke to whom and what it was about. A quick glance at the coding in the LANGUAGE column tells you whether the child spoke much or little. The coding tells you how much he was talking with other children and how much with adults, and whether he initiated talk or mainly responded to others.

The task code (what the child *does*)

These categories describe the child's behaviour — what he was actually doing each minute. They include play behaviour such as *pretend, art,* or *manipulation*, as well as non-play behaviour such as *watching* or *cruising*.

Why Code?

You may think that your narrative records in the ACTIVITY and LANGUAGE columns might be enough for you to see what went on in your observation. But the coding is a way of *summarizing* these large amounts of detail about what was done and said. It enables you to see at a glance the *structure* of a child's activity over the observation. With just the narrative record there is so much detailed information that you may not be able to see the wood for the trees!

So from the coding you can read off rapidly what activities the child engaged in, how long he spent in each one, whether he was alone or with other children or adults for most of the time, whether he was speaking with the others or just silently playing beside them. And you may be able to see whether being alone tends to go with some kinds of activity, while interacting with others goes with different activities.

How to Code

Go through your observation and for each minute choose the appropriate categories from the coding lists — these lists are given in the following pages. Look at the sample observation (Figure A1.3) at the end for help with the layout. Make sure that you have completed the coding for each minute, in each of the three types of code.

Using the Social Code

For each minute, code whether the child's activity was:

SOL   Solitary.
PAIR Two people together (target child plus one other child or adult).
SG   In a small group of three to five children.
LG   In a large group of six or more children.

Sometimes, in a group of two or more children, the child appears to have little contact with the others. If he is playing or working on his own, despite the others around him, add a /P, for 'parallel' to the *social code*.
For instance:

PAIR/P   means that the child is near another but not playing or talking with him.
LG/P   means that the child sits or stands in a large group of children but does not interact with any of them.

Note that the children may even be doing the same thing, but call it /P if they are not interacting with one another.

Special mention of the adult:

Put a circle around the *social code* if the child is interacting with, or is very near to, an *adult*. So,

⟨PAIR⟩   would be the code if the child is chatting with a helper.
SG/P   might be the code if the child is sitting next to an adult who is supervising a group activity.

Figure A1.3: Sample record, coded

CHILD'S INITIALS: **A.N.** SEX: **boy** AGE: **4/11** DATE AND TIME OBSERVED: **18/11 10·50 am**			
ACTIVITY RECORD	LANGUAGE RECORD	TASK	SOCIAL
¹ TC at woodwork table, hammers nail into wood. Goes round table & looks at small metal pieces. Offers nail to A.	TC → A: Will you bang this? A → TC (bangs nail in)	SSC	PAIR
² Watches A carefully. Gives A a bottle cap to hammer on for him	A → TC (about hammering) TC → A (asks her to hammer on cap)	SSC	PAIR
³ Watches A hammering his bottle cap & milk bottle top into wood with nail. A finishes - hands TC his wood. (looks like		SSC	PAIR
⁴ Carries woodwork outside, back indoors. Takes it to paint. Paints it blue, with brush		ART	SOL
⁵ Paints his woodwork. Paints, wipes thumb on paper, on wood.		ART	SOL
⁶ Paints his woodwork.		ART	SOL
⁷ Takes coat off - gets apron and puts it on. Continues to paint	A → TC: Not with your coat on, you'll get it all over	ART	SOL
⁸ Paints woodwork	A → TC: Now finish that and come and have your milk. TC → A: No! A → TC: We'll leave some then	ART	PAIR
⁹ Looks at hands - goes to washbowl in corner (leaves woodwork on paint table) · Washes with I C	TC ⟷ C TC ⟷ C A → TC + C (about washing)	DA	PAIR
¹⁰ Washes hands, dries them Goes to sit at milk table, next to twin brother Helper gives him cup	TC → A: Where's mine? I haven't got a cup. TC → C: I got a blue one	DA	LG

If the child's social situation changes within the minute, decide which was the longest type of interaction and code the whole minute as that. For example, if the child has a short chat with a friend but plays alone for most of the minute, code this as SOL and not PAIR.

However, it is useful to make a special note of *any* contact with an adult, even if it is very short — you still put a circle around the *social code*. (This helps you keep track of the effect of the adults.) So if the child was playing alone except for a brief exchange of greetings with a passing helper, the *social code* would be SOL for that minute.

Using the Language Code

The method of coding the language has already been explained under 'Recording your observation' in the LANGUAGE column. If you have already used the abbreviations listed on page 3 (TC→C; S→TC: and so on), then you have already coded the language! So just make sure that you have indeed completed this coding.

Using the Task Code

For each minute of observation write down the appropriate *task code* category. There is a list of these categories and their abbreviations on the following pages.

As in the *social code*, you note only the more prominent behaviour if the child engages in more than one category of behaviour in a minute. If, in a minute, a child shows two different sorts of behaviour one after the other, decide which was the longest and code it all as that. If the child engages in two sorts of behaviour at the same time (for example, *manipulation* together with *watching*), decide which seemed the main one and code it all as that.

You have already marked the start and end of the themes in the child's activity by drawing double lines across the page. Often the theme and the *task coding* coincide, so that when you change to a new *task code* category the theme changes too. But sometimes one theme could include more than one *task code* category, or one *task code* series could contain more than one theme. Look at the fully-coded sample observation at the end, and at the examples given under 'looking for themes' on page 233, where the themes and *task code* categories overlap each other.

The Task Code Categories

Each of the categories below may include talk. Sometimes it may appear that social interaction is more important to the child than the task, but this is acknowledged in the *social code*. If there is an appropriate task code, it should be used.

Large muscle movement (LMM): Active movement of the child's body, requiring coordination of larger muscles, such as running, climbing.

Large scale construction (LSC): Arranging and building dens, trains, etc., with large crates, blocks, etc.

Small scale construction (SSC): Using small constructional materials such as lego, meccano, hammering and nailing.

Art (ART): 'Free expression' creative activities such as painting, drawing, chalking, cutting, sticking.

Manipulation (MAN): The mastering or refining of manual skills requiring coordination of the hand/arm and the senses: e.g., handling sand, dough, clay, water, etc. Also sewing, gardening, arranging and sorting objects.

Adult-directed art and manipulation (ADM): The child is mastering and refining skills and techniques under adult direction, and sometimes with an adult-determined end-product; e.g., tracing, directed collage.

Structured materials (SM): The use of materials, with design constraints, e.g. jigsaw puzzles, peg-boards, templates, picture or shape matching materials, counting boards, shape posting boxes, bead-threading and sewing cards.

Three Rs Activities (3Rs): Attempts at reading, writing or counting. It includes attentive looking at books.

Examination (EX): Careful examination of an object or material, e.g. looking through a magnifying glass. It differs from *manipulation* in that the looking, smelling or tasting is more important than the handling.

Problem-solving (PS): The child solves a 'problem' in a purposeful way using logical reasoning; e.g., looking to see why something won't work and then repairing it.

Pretend (PRE): The transformation of everyday objects, people or events so that their 'meaning' takes precedence over 'reality'.

Scale-version toys (SVT): Arranging miniature objects, e.g., dolls' houses, farm and zoo sets, transport toys, toy forts. It does not include use of toys such as prams, dolls and dishes. If miniature objects are used in pretend play, use previous category

Informal games (IG): A play situation, with or without language, where the child is playing an informal game with another child. These are spontaneously and loosely organized; e.g., following one another around while chanting, hiding in a corner and giggling, or holding hands and jumping.

Games with rules (GWR): Includes ball games, skittles, circle games including singing games, and board games such as snakes and ladders, dominoes, noughts and crosses, etc.

Music (MUS): Listening to sounds, rhythms or music, playing instruments, singing solos and dancing.

Passive adult-led group activities (PALGA): A large group of children, under the leadership of an adult, listen to stories, rhymes or finger plays, watch television, watch a planned demonstration (e.g., nature table, making popcorn), etc.

Social interaction, non-play (SINP): Social interaction, with another child or with an adult, verbal or physical, but definitely not play, with another child or with an adult. E.g., chatting, borrowing, seeking or giving help or information to someone, aggressive behaviour (not play-fighting), teasing, being cuddled or comforted by an adult. Note that *social interaction, non-play* is used only when the child is not engaged in another task code category; e.g., if he is doing a puzzle while chatting to a friend, code it as *structured materials*.

Distress behaviour (DB): Seeking comfort or attention from adult or other child. He must show visible signs of distress or make a visible bid for comfort; e.g., prolonged crying, wanton destruction of materials, social withdrawal.

Standing around, aimless wander or gaze (SA/AWG): The child is not actively engaged in a task or watching a specific event.

Cruise (CR): Active movement around from one thing to another, or purposeful looking around, when the child appears to be searching for something to do.

Purposeful movement (PM): Purposeful movement towards an object, person or place: e.g., searching for an object, going outdoors, crossing the room to another activity.

Wait (W): The child's time of inactivity while waiting, for adult or child.

Watching (WA): Watching other people or events. The child may watch a specific person or activity, or look around in general. Includes listening-in to conversations without participating.

Domestic activity (DA): Includes going to the toilet, hand-washing, dressing, arrival and departure, rest, tidying up, milk, snack or meal.

Appendix B

Statements on Assessment

1. 'Assessment is seen as the process of gathering information. The means by which this is achieved will be many and varied. The information gathered may well serve a variety of purposes, but the most important will be the influence it has on teachers' decisions about the needs of the children in his/her class and the learning opportunities which need to be planned.' (Bennett and Hewett, 1989)

2. 'Tests have an important place in the range of assessments used by teachers. On occasion tests provide unique data which other forms of assessment are not designed to yield. Importantly, tests may be the most efficient and fair means of assessment of several available methods. These conditions may not always prevail, so teachers and other users will need to be alert to the issues and be prepared to obtain data from trials in order to base evaluations of particular approaches on evidence rather than assertion.

   'Using tests properly demands a certain understanding about their base in theory or the curriculum and rationales which connect these with pupils' circumstances and teachers' purposes. A critical point is the variable nature of measurement, arising from the necessity to draw samples, of questions and responses, of pupils and of occasions.' (Sumner, 1987)

3. 'Assessment in education has been critized for interfering with the process of learning, the analogy being that of a gardener constantly pulling up his plants to see if the roots are growing. There is some truth in this, particularly if there is too much assessment of the wrong kind, but it also distorts reality to make a point. Gardeners do

have to find out if their plants are growing and they do this, not by uprooting them, but by careful observation with a knowledgeable eye, so that they can give water and food at the right time and avoid either undernourishment or over-watering.' (Wynne Harlen, 1983)

4. 'Teachers make assessments all the time; sometimes they are full and formal, resulting in a mark, a grade, or a certificate. But they are often a matter of the moment, a check as to who is keeping up with the work, and the reward is no more than a smile or a frown, a nod of the head or an encouraging word . . . In our view assessment is part and parcel of the teacher's service to pupils, not merely as motivation and reward, but as direct contribution to the children's growing awareness and appreciation of themselves.' (Bentley and Malvern, 1982)

5. 'When trying to establish the worth of anything, and hence to evaluate it, we need information and we need yardsticks against which to judge not only the information we require, but the information we receive. In education, where we are concerned with the worth of such things as curricula, teaching methods and course materials, one major significant source of information, although not the only one, is the performance of those being taught — the pupils. We, therefore, need to look for methods both formal and informal of assessing their performance.' (Frith and Macintosh, 1984)

6. 'Education is a complex process involving the selection of ideas (concepts, values and skills) and the planning of experience designed to foster mastery of those ideas in the people subject to the educational system programme. Choices must be made in the planning of the education programme, and the effectiveness of the programme must also be studied. Evaluation is, therefore, inevitable in education.' (P. L. Dressel, 1976)

7. 'Assessment should be frequent, otherwise learners will not receive the feedback which is so vital to success. Assessment should also be timely, so that the pupil appreciates its relevance. Much assessment can best be done alongside and with pupil involvement; formative profiling is a good example of this process. Assessments should be used to shape the type and level of work for each pupil. Regular self-assessment by teachers should be encouraged.' (HMSO, 1985)

8. 'We lack broad agreement about how to describe and scrutinize the primary curriculum. The absence of clarity and agreement about what children should be capable of at various stages of their primary education leads to a distinct lack of information about standards of pupils' achievement in individual primary schools and a consequent difficulty of establishing standards of achievements as a basis for assessment of performance.' (Bolton, 1985)

9. 'The word "assessment" is from the latin *assidere*, to sit beside. Sitting beside children suggests a close relationship and a sharing of experience. It is ironic therefore to find that educational assessment is associated in many people's minds with two contrasting interpretations. First there is hard-nosed objectivity, an obsession with the measurement of performances...and an increasingly technical vocabulary which defies most teachers save for the determined few with time on their hands. Secondly, and to many others, assessment presents a very different face as the means by which schools and teachers — wittingly or unwittingly — sort out children for occupations of different status and remuneration in a hierarchically ordered society.' (Satterly, 1989)

Bibliography

ABERCROMBIE, M. L. J. (1969) *The Anatomy of Judgement*, Harmondsworth, Penguin Books.

ADAMS, E. and BURGESS, T. (1989) Teachers' Own Records: A System Promoting Professional Quality, Oxford, NFER-Nelson.

ADAMS, R. S. and BIDDLE, B. J. (1970) *Realities of Teaching: Explorations with Videotape*, New York, Holt, Rinehart and Winston.

AINSCOW, M. (1988) 'Beyond the eyes of the monster: an analysis of recent trends in assessment and recording', *Support for Learning*, 3, 3, pp. 149–53.

AINSCOW, M. and CONNER, C. (1990) *School-based Inquiry: Notes and Background Reading*, Cambridge, England, Cambridge Institute of Education.

ARMSTRONG, M., (1980) *Closely Observed Children: The Diary of a Primary Classroom*, London, Chameleon Books.

ARMSTRONG, M., (1988) 'Popular Education and the National Curriculum', *Forum*, **30**, 3, pp. 74–6.

BASSEY, M. (1990) *Trent Assessment Guide for Primary Schools: National Curriculum Key Stage One*, Department of Primary Education, Nottingham Polytechnic, London, Local Education Authority Publications (LEAP).

BELL, J. (1987) *Doing Your Research Project. A Guide for First-time Researchers in Education and Social Science*, Milton Keynes, Open University Press.

BENNETT, N. and DESFORGES, C., COCKBURN, A. and WILKINSON, B. (1984) *The Quality of Pupil Learning Experiences*, London, Lawrence Erlbaum Associates.

BENTLEY, C. and MALVERN, D. (1983) *Guides to Assessment in Education; Mathematics*, London, Macmillan Education.

BICKER, H. (1950) 'Using anecdotal records to know the child', in *Fostering Mental Health in Our School, 1950 Yearbook*, Washington, DC, Association for Supervision and Curriculum Development, National Education Association.

BLACK, H., DEVINE, M. and TURNER, E. (1989) *Aspects of Assessment: A Primary Perspective*, Edinburgh, Schools Assessment Research and Support Unit, Scottish Council for Research in Education.

BLYTH, W. A. L. (1990) *Making the Grade for Primary Humanities*, Milton Keynes, Open University Press.

BOLTON, E. (1986) 'Assessment techniques and approaches: an overview', in *Better Schools (Evaluation and Appraisal Conference, Birmingham, Nov. 1985)*, London, HMSO.

BRANDT, R. M. (1972) *Studying behaviour in natural settings*, New York, Holt, Rinehart and Winston.

BRIGHOUSE, T. (1988) 'Competing with yourself can be tougher than tests', *The Times Educational Supplement*, 30 September, p. 17.

BROADFOOT, P. and OSBORN, M. (1987) 'French lessons', *The Times Educational Supplement*, 3 July.

BROADFOOT, P. (1988) 'The National Curriculum Framework and Records of Achievement', TORRANCE, H. (Ed.) *National Assessment and Testing: A Research Response, papers presented to the BERA Conference, 11 Feb. 1988*.

BROADFOOT, P., GRANT, M., JAMES, M., NUTTALL, D. and STIERER, B. (1989) *Interim report of the National Evaluation of Extension work in Records of Achievement Schemes*, DES and Welsh Office.

CALOUSTE GULBENKIAN FOUNDATION (1982) *The Arts in Schools*, London, Oyez Press.

CENTRAL ADVISORY COUNCIL FOR EDUCATION (England) (1967) *Children and their Primary Schools*, (*Plowden Report*), London, HMSO (2 vols.).

CHISHOLM, L., (1987) "Vorsprung ex machina? Aspects of Curriculum and assessment in cultural comparison', *Journal of Educational Policy*, 2, 2, pp. 149–59.

CHITTY, C. (1988) 'Two models of National Curriculum: origins and interpretation', in LAWTON, D. and CHITTY, C. (Eds.) *The National Curriculum, Bedford Way papers, No. 33*, London, University of London Institute of Education.

CHRISTIE, T. (1990) 'Plan Feedback', *The Times Educational Supplement*, 16 March.

CLIFT, P., WEINER, G. and WILSON, E. (1981) *Record Keeping in the Primary School*, London, Macmillan.

COHEN, L. and MARION, L. (1985) *Research Methods in Education*, London, Croom Helm.

CONNER, C. (1988) 'Testing, testing, testing', *Primary File*, 4, pp. 35–8.

CONNER, C. (1990) 'National Curriculum Assessment and the Primary School — reactions and illustrations of emerging practice', *The Curriculum Journal*, Vol. 1, No. 2, Autumn.

CROLL, P. (1986) *Systematic Classroom Observation*, Basingstoke, Falmer Press.

CROLL, P. (1990) *Norm and Criterion-referenced Assessment: Some Reflections in the Context of Assessment and Testing in the National Curriculum*, *Redland Papers No. 1*, Bristol Polytechnic Faculty of Education.

CROWLEY, C. (1988) 'Primary School Shakespeare: A Cross-curriculum Mode of Learning', unpublished Advanced Diploma Long Study, Cambridge Institute of Education.

DEAL, T. E. and BOLMAN, L. G. (1984) *Modern Approaches to Understanding and Managing Organisation*, New York, Jossey-Bass.

DEAN, J. (1983) *Organising Learning in the Primary School*, London, Croom Helm.

DEAN, J. (1990) *Organising Learning in the Primary School*, Second Edition, London, Routledge: forthcoming.

DES (1984) *Records of Achievement: a Statement of Policy*, London, HMSO.

DES (1987) *The National Curriculum 5–16: a Consultation Document*, London, HMSO, July.

DES (1988) *National Curriculum Task Group on Assessment and Testing. A Report*, London, HMSO.

DES (1988) *National Curriculum Task Group on Assessment and Testing: Three Supplementary Reports*, London, HMSO.

DES (1988) *National Curriculum. Task Group on Assessment and Testing Report. A Digest for Schools*, London, HMSO.

DES (1990) *The Education (Individual Pupils' Achievements) Regulations 1990, Draft Regulations*, London, HMSO.

DES (1990) *Standards in Education 1988–89. The Annual Report of HM Senior Chief Inspector Schools*, London, HMSO.

DES (1990) *The Education (National Curriculum) Assessment Arrangements in English, Maths and Science, Draft Orders*. London, HMSO.

DONALDSON, M. (1978) *Children's Minds*, London, Fontana Books.

DRESSELL, P. L. (1976) *Handbook of Academic Evaluation*, New York, Jossey-Bass.

DRUMMOND, M. J. (1989) Paper presented to Cambridge Institute Course M4, 'Assessment and Testing in the Primary School', Nov. 1989.

DUNCAN, A. and DUNN, W. (1988) *What Primary Teachers Should Know About Assessment*, London, Hodder and Stoughton.

ELLIOTT, J. (1983) 'Searching for Meaning', OU Course E364. Curriculum Evaluation and Assessment in Educational Institutions. Milton Keynes.

ESSEX LEA (1989) 'Essex Assessment Initiative Primary Children's Assessment', resource folder for primary teachers, Essex LEA.

FLANDERS, N. (1970) *Analysing Teacher Behaviour*, Reading, Mass., Addison-Wesley.

FORSYTH, K. and WOOD, J. (undated) 'Ways of doing research in one's own classroom', Ford Teaching Project, pp. 14–15.

FRITH, D. S. and MACINTOSH, H. G. (1984) *A Teacher's Guide to Assessment*, Cheltenham, Stanley Thornes.

FULLAN, M. (1984) *The Meaning of Educational Change*, New York, Teachers College Press.

GALTON, M., SIMON, B. and CROLL, P. (1980) *Inside the Primary Classroom*, London, Routledge and Kegan Paul.

GIBSON, R. (1986) 'Teacher–parent Communication' — HOLBEIN in (GOULDING, S., BELL, J., BUSH, T., FOX, A., GOODEY, J.) *Case Studies in Educational Management*, London, Harper and Row.

GIPPS, C. (1988) 'What Exams Would Mean for Primary Education', in LAWTON, D. and CHITTY, C. (Eds.) *The National Curriculum, Bedford Way Paper 33*, London, University of London, Institute of Education.

GIPPS, C. (1990) 'Assessment is Unattainable', *The Times Educational Supplement*, 2 March, p. 27.

GIPPS, C., STEADMAN, S., BLACKSTONE, T. and STIERER, B. (1983) *Testing Children: Standardised Testing in Schools and LEAs*, London, Heinemann.

GIPPS, C., CROSS, H. and GOLDSTEIN, H. (1987) *Warnock's 18 percent: Children with Special Needs in the Primary School*, Lewes, Falmer Press.

GIPPS, C. and GOLDSTEIN, H. (1989) 'A Curriculum for teacher assessment', *Journal of Curriculum Studies*, 21, 6, pp. 561–5.

GRIFFIN-BEALE (Ed.) (1984) *Christian Schiller: In His Own Words*, London, NAPE.

HARGREAVES, D. (1990) 'Assessing the alternatives', *The Times Educational Supplement*, 15 April, p. A18.

HARLEN, W. (1977) *Match and Mismatch*, Edinburgh, Oliver and Boyd.

HARLEN, W. (1983) *Guides to Assessment in Education Science*, London, Macmillan Education.

HARLEN, W. (Ed.) (1985) *Primary Science taking the Plunge. How to Teach Primary Science More Effectively*, London, Heinemann.

HARTNETT, A. and NAISH, M. (1990) 'The Sleep of Reason Breeds Monsters: The Birth of a Statutory Curriculum in England and Wales', *Journal of Curriculum Studies*, 22, 1, pp. 1–6.

HEWETT, P. and BENNETT, M. K. (1989) *Assessment of Learning. A Hertfordshire Primary Context. A Report Arising from the Secondment of two Primary Headteachers*. Herts LEA.

HILLINGDON, LONDON BOROUGH OF (1985) *Assessment INSET*, Hillingdon Assessment Support team.

HITCHCOCK, G. and HUGHES, D. (1989) *Research and the Teacher: A Qualitative Introduction to School Based Research*, London, Routledge and Kegan Paul.

HMSO (1986) *Third Report from the Education Science and Arts Committee: Achievement in Primary Schools*, London, HMSO.

HOLLY, M. L. (1989) *Writing to Grow*, Portsmouth, USA, Heinemann.

HOLLY, P. (1989a) *School-Based Development for Flexible Learning. Harnessing the Power of Whole-school Approaches*, Cambridge, UK, IMTEC.

HOLLY, P. (1989b) *School-based Development in Action, School-based Development Working Paper 1*, Cambridge, UK, IMTEC.

HOLLY, P. (1990) 'From Teaching Schools to Learning Schools', in BRIDGES, D. (Ed.) *Teaching to Learning*, forthcoming publication.

HOOK, C. (1985) *Studying Classrooms*, Deakin, Australia, Deakin University Press.

HOLT, M. (1987) 'Bureaucratic Benefits', *The Times Educational Supplement*, 18 September, p. 30.

HOPKINS, D. (1985) *A Teacher's Guide to Classroom Research*, Milton Keynes, Open University Press.

HOPKINS, D. (1988) 'Why National Testing is wrong', Cambridge, UK, *Cambridge Institute of Education, Newsletter* 9.

INKSON, G. (1987) 'Profiling in the Primary School', *Primary Teaching Studies*, 3, 1, pp. 98–107.

INNER LONDON EDUCATION AUTHORITY (1985) *Improving Primary Schools. The Report of the Committee on Primary Education*, chaired by Norman Thomas, London.

INNER LONDON EDUCATION AUTHORITY (1989) *The Primary Language Record Handbook for Teachers*. London, ILEA Centre for Language in Primary Education, Webber Row.

INNER LONDON EDUCATION AUTHORITY (1990) *The Primary Language Record and the National Curriculum*, London, ILEA Centre for Language in Primary Education, Webber Row.

IRELAND, D. and RUSSELL, T. (1978) 'Pattern Analysis as Used in the Ottawa Valley Teaching Project', *CARN Newsletter*, No. 21. Cambridge, UK, Cambridge Institute of Education.

ISLE OF WIGHT TEACHERS' CENTRE (1988) *Topic Work How and Why?* Isle of Wight Teachers' Centre.

JARDINE, R. (1972) 'An Exploration in the Use of Video-recording in Teacher–pupil Relationships', *Visual Education*, March, pp. 21–7.

LAMBERT, D. (Ed.) (1990) *Teacher Assessment and National Curriculum Geography*, Sheffield, Assessment and Examinations Working Group of the Geographical Association.

LAW, P. (1986) *Records of Pupil Achievement: A Case Study of Thomas Mills High School*, Suffolk County Council.

LAWTON, D. and CHITTY, C. (1988) 'Introduction', in LAWTON, D. and CHITTY, C. (Eds.) *The National Curriculum*, Bedford Way Papers No. 33, London, University of London Institute of Education.

LAWTON, D. (1989) 'Measure of Doubt', *The Times Educational Supplement*, January.

LINCOLN, Y. S. and GUBA, E. G. (1981) 'Do Evaluators Wear Grass Skirts? Going Native and Ethnocentrism as Problems in Utilisation', paper presented at the joint annual meeting of the Evaluation network and the Evaluation Research Society, Austin, Texas.

MACINTOSH, H. G. and HALE, D. E. (1976) *Assessment and the Secondary School Teacher*, London, Routledge and Kegan Paul.

MARSHALL, P. (1986) 'The role and responsibility of the school: an overview', in *Better Schools* (Evaluation and Appraisal Conference, Birmingham, November 1985), London, HMSO.

MCGREW, W. C. (1972) *An Ethological Study of Children's Behaviour*, New York, Academic Press.

MCNAMARA, D. (1988) 'In Place of teaching', *The Times Educational Supplement*, 28 October, p. 16.

MEHAN, H. (1973) 'Assessing children's language-using abilities: methodological and cross cultural implications', in ARMER, M. and GRIMSHAW, A. D. (Eds.)

Comparative Social Research: Methodological Problems and Strategies, New York, Wiley.

MURPHY, R. and TORRANCE, H. (1988) *The Changing Face of Educational Assessment*, Milton Keynes, Open University Press.

NATIONAL CURRICULUM COUNCIL (1989) *An Introduction to the National Curriculum*, York, NCC in association with the Open University.

NATIONAL CURRICULUM COUNCIL (1989) *Developing INSET Activities*, York, NCC in association with the Open University.

NEWSON, J. and NEWSON, E. (1976) 'Parental Roles and Social Contexts', in SHIPMAN, M.D. (Ed.), *The Organisation and Impact of Social Research*, London, Routledge and Kegan Paul.

NUTTALL, D.L. (1987) 'Testing, testing, testing', *NUT Education Review*, 1, 2, pp. 32–5.

POLLARD, A. (1987) 'Social Differentiation in Primary Schools', in DADDS, M. (Ed.) *Of Primary Concern, Cambridge Journal of Education*, 17, 3, pp. 158–61.

POWELL, R.A. (1990) 'Who gave us a false start on assessments?' *The Times Educational Supplement*, 23 March.

QUALTER, A. (1988) 'Serving Many Purposes. Aggregating Scores: Does it Work?' *Curriculum*, 9, 3, pp. 159–64.

REID, J.A. (1984) 'A Journal for the Teacher', in *Children Writing*: A Reader, Deakin, Australia, Course ECT 418 Deakin University.

REY, M. (1988) 'Vive la difference!', *The Times Educational Supplement*, 28 October.

RICHARDS, C. (1984) *The Study of Primary Education*, Vol. 2, Lewes, Falmer Press.

RICHARDSON, T. (1989) 'Approaches to Personal Development in the Primary School', in *Whole Person: Whole School, Bridging the Academic–Pastoral Divide*. London, National Association for Pastoral Care in Education, SCDC Publication, Longmans.

ROWLAND, S. (1984) *The Enquiring Classroom*, Lewes, Falmer.

ROWLAND, S. (1986) 'Classroom Enquiry: An Approach to Understanding Children', in HUSTLER, D., CASSIDY, T. and CUFF, T. *Action Research in Classrooms and Schools*, London, Allen and Unwin.

ROWNTREE, D. (1977) *Assessing Students. How Shall We Know Them?* London, Harper and Row.

RUDDOCK, J. and HOPKINS, D. (Eds.) (1985) *Research as a Basis for Teaching*, London, Heinemann.

SATTERLY, D. (1989) *Assessment in Schools*, 2nd ed., Oxford, Basil Blackwell.

SCHAEFFER, R. (1967) *The School as a Centre of Inquiry*, New York, Harper and Row.

SCHOOLS COUNCIL (1971) *Choosing a Curriculum for the Young School Leaver, Working Paper No. 33*, London, Evans/Methuen.

SCHOOLS EXAMINATIONS AND ASSESSMENT COUNCIL (1989) *National Curriculum Assessment Arrangements*, July.

SCHOOLS EXAMINATIONS AND ASSESSMENT COUNCIL (1989) 'National Curriculum Assessment. Record Keeping and Inservice Training', *SEAC Recorder*, **2**, Summer, p. 1.

SCHOOLS EXAMINATIONS AND ASSESSMENT COUNCIL (1989) *National Curriculum: Assessment Arrangements (2)*, December.

SCHOOLS EXAMINATIONS AND ASSESSMENT COUNCIL (1990) 'National Curriculum Assessment', *SEAC Recorder*, **5**.

SHIPMAN, M. (1983) *Assessment in Primary and Middle Schools*, London, Croom Helm.

SIMON, B. (1981) 'The Primary School Revolution, Myth or Reality?' in GALTON, M., SIMON, B. and WILLCOCKS, J. (Eds.) *Research and Practice in the Primary Classroom*, London, Routledge and Kegan Paul.

SIMONS, H. (1988) *Teacher Professionalism and the National Curriculum: Bedford Way paper 33*, London, University of London Institute of Education.

SIMPSON, M. (1990) 'Why Criterion-referenced Assessment will not Improve the Quality of Learning', *The Curriculum Journal*, **1**, 2, September.

SUMNER, R. (1987) *The Role of Testing in Schools*, Windsor, NFER-Nelson.

SUTTON, R. (1990) 'Issues for Teachers in Implementing National Curriculum Geography', in LAMBERT, D. (Ed.) *Teacher Assessment and National Curriculum Geography*, Sheffield, Geographical Association.

SYLVA, K., ROY, C. and PAINTER, M. (1980) *Child-watching at Playgroup and Nursery School*, London, McIntyre.

THOMAS, N. (1990) *Primary Education from Plowden to the 1990s*, Basingstoke, Falmer Press.

THOMPSON, P. (1989) 'Extenuating circumstances', *The Independent*, 13 April.

WALKER, R. (1985) *Doing Research. A Handbook for Teachers*, London, Methuen.

WALKER, R. and ADELMAN, C. (1975) *A Guide to Classroom Observation*, London, Methuen.

WHALLEY, D. (1989) 'TGAT is torn apart', *The Times Educational Supplement*, 25 August.

WRAGG, T. (1990) 'Who Put the Ass in Assessment?' *The Times Educational Supplement*, 16 February.

WRIGHTSTONE, J. W. (1960) 'Observation techniques', in HARRIS, C. W. and LIBA, M. R. (Eds.) *Encyclopedia of Educational Research*, 3rd ed., New York, Macmillan.

ZIMMERMAN, D. H. and WIEDER, D. L. (1977) 'The Diary-interview Method', *Urban Life*, **5**, 4, January, pp. 479–99.

Index